Decolonizing Educational Leadership

Ann E. Lopez

Decolonizing Educational Leadership

Exploring Alternative Approaches
to Leading Schools

Ann E. Lopez
Ontario Institute for Studies in Education
University of Toronto
Toronto, ON, Canada

ISBN 978-3-030-62379-1   ISBN 978-3-030-62380-7   (eBook)
https://doi.org/10.1007/978-3-030-62380-7

This Palgrave Macmillan imprint is published by the registered company Springer Nature Switzerland AG.
The registered company address is: Gewerbestrasse 11, 6330 Cham, Switzerland

I dedicate this book to my mother, father, grandmother, aunts, uncles, and ancestors—some of whom are still with us and some who have crossed over. I also dedicate this book to all educators fighting for justice and freedom from oppression.

ACKNOWLEDGMENTS

I would like to acknowledge all the people who have contributed to my educational journey and made this book possible—family, friends, scholars, and colleagues. This book was possible because of their kindness and generosity extended to me. To the scholars who have laid the ground work and foundation on which this work stands. To my grandmother who always showed empathy, love, and care to everyone and encouraged me to speak out against injustice. Thanks to my family—daughter, grand daughters, sisters, brother, aunts, uncles, cousins—who provided me with love, support, and encouragement over the years. Thank you for your encouragement.

Thanks to my research collaborators. Thanks to Professor Njoki Wane, my friend and colleague, who took me on my first trip to Kenya and the continent of Africa. Thanks to my ancestors whose spirits are always present and are a source of strength. Sankofa, the African word from the Akan tribe in Ghana, reminds us of the importance of reaching back and reclaiming our past, so we can move forward and understand why and how we came to be who we are today.

To my granddaughters and all children, you are the focus of this work.

CONTENTS

ABOUT THE AUTHOR

Ann E. Lopez is a professor in the Department of Leadership, Higher and Adult Education in the Educational Leadership and Policy Program. Lopez is a scholar with wide public education experience as a former secondary school teacher and administrator in one of Canada's largest school boards located in the Greater Toronto Area. Her scholarship focuses on anti-racist education, culturally responsive leadership, decolonizing education, equity and diversity, and school leadership. Her most recent publications include "Anti-Black Racism in Education: A School Leader's Journey of Resistance and Hope" in *Handbook on Promoting Social Justice in Education*; "Language, Diversity and Culturally Responsive Education" in *Migration and Language Education*; "Dialogue and Praxis: Re-Conceptualizing Multicultural Education as a Decolonizing Effort" in *Multicultural Perspectives*. She is the co-editor of *Transformative Pedagogies for Teacher Education* and the author of *Culturally Responsive and Socially Just Leadership: From Theory to Action*. Lopez has written several book chapters and journal articles, and has presented her research locally and globally. She is the Co-Editor-in-Chief of the *Journal of School Leadership* and Co-Series Editor, *Studies in Educational Administration*. Lopez is the Director of the Centre for Leadership and Diversity at the University of Toronto and Provostial Advisor on Access Programs since 2017. Lopez was the Academic Director of Initial Teacher Education and the Concurrent Teacher Education Program from 2013 to 2016. She was the President of the National Association for Multicultural Education (NAME) from 2018 to 2020 and the 2015 recipient of the NAME Multicultural Educator of the Year Award. Lopez is the 2020 recipient of the Award for Distinguished Contributions to Teaching at the Ontario Institute for Studies in Education, University of Toronto.

LIST OF FIGURES

CHAPTER 1

Introduction: Toward a Theory of Decolonizing Educational Leadership

Abstract This chapter situates this volume in my ontological experiences, professionally and personally. It examines ways in which education and schooling embrace social organizing practices grounded in the knowledge of colonizers. It explores ways in which education continues to be a colonial project and the manifestations of settler colonialism present in everyday schooling practices. It situates the book and notions of decolonizing educational leadership in current social and political contexts and movements for social change. This chapter highlights focus of the subsequent chapters in this volume which includes challenges and possibilities of educational leadership, coloniality, decolonizing the mind, restoring capcity, re-centering and reconnecting, and moving forward.

Keywords Positionality • Colonial project • Colonialism • Settler colonialism

I spent eighteen years as a secondary classroom teacher and school administrator before being hired fulltime into academia. The last three of those eighteen years I spent as a seconded instructor[1] in the Bachelor of Education program at the Ontario Institute for Studies in Education (OISE). Over

---

[1] Seconded instructors in Ontario are public school teachers or administrators on loan to Bachelor of Education programs in the province.

A. E. Lopez, *Decolonizing Educational Leadership*, https://doi.org/10.1007/978-3-030-62380-7_1

1

those eighteen years I have seen some teachers and administrators being agentive in responding to the needs of Black, Indigenous, and People of Color (BIPOC) students and some outrightly engaging in racist behaviors. Students also shared stories about their experiences. When I became an administrator, I saw the impact of leadership on the overall schooling experiences of students. This went beyond pedagogy to the areas of discipline, school culture, hiring of teachers, allocation of resources, and basically all activities that take place in a school. I also witnessed oppressive leadership practices where Black and Brown students were given harsher suspensions, the so-called good kid—which often was a White student—got a slap on the wrist, while Black students were given in-school suspensions or sent home. I witnessed the harsh tone in which some parents were spoken to, and the 'policing' of primarily Black students. At the last school where I worked as an administrator before being seconded to OISE, most of the students had an Individual Education Plan (IEP), and were predominantly Black boys, poor White students, many of whom were labeled behavioral, and sent to the contact room for support. Through these experiences I realized the impact that school leaders can make on students' educational outcomes and lives, and the possibilities for challenging discrimination and oppression through intentional leadership practices.

As I reflect on schooling practices and engage in research with school leaders in different contexts the continued presence of coloniality in education is evident. This includes discrimination, oppression, and exclusion based on aspects of students' intersecting identities such as ability, class, social economic status, language, religion, race, sexuality, and other markers of identity; ways in which knowledge and power are embedded in policies and the organizational structures of schools; and silencing of some groups. The continued presence of coloniality in schooling, colonial and hegemonic narratives, is not only present in Western countries but also in former colonies and the Global South. Scholars such as Marie Battiste, Linda Tuhiwai Smith, Albert Memmi, and others point to ways in which schooling and education is used as a vehicle to perpetuate colonialism in many forms long after physical colonial domination has ended. My earlier works were framed through social justice and culturally responsive leadership theorizing, where coloniality was not foregrounded. In this volume, I am arguing that the presence of coloniality in education must be named and disrupted in all aspects of schooling, and in particular educational and school leadership through decolonizing education; and for school leaders to be supported to take up, engage in, and advance this work.

POSITIONALITY

I am a Black woman born and raised in Jamaica—a former British colony. My experiences growing up and education were informed by the colonial education system installed in Jamaica by the British. I was also impacted by my grandmother who was a constant presence in her grandchildren's lives. She was kind and caring to everyone and had words of wisdom for every situation. She nurtured my love for reading and shared numerous stories that were passed down to her from her parents and grandparents. Through these stories I became interested in learning more about Jamaica's history, and my ancestors. As a child growing up, I was fascinated with the stories of the enslaved who had fought British rule such as Nanny of the Maroons rebel leader and Jamaican National Hero. I also read about the decimation of the Arawak Indians (also called Tainos)—the Indigenous people of Jamaica—by the Europeans. They came from South America and named the island Xaymaca, which meant "land of wood and water." These stories planted a seed and desire to learn more about my African ancestors, a history that was not taught in school. This interest was further peaked when I entered the University of the West Indies, Mona Campus in Kingston, and engaged with the work of Walter Rodney, Frantz Fanon, and other postcolonial scholars. The former Prime Minister of Jamaica Michael Manley, also a postcolonial scholar, raised the impact and legacy of colonialism not only on the island of Jamaica but former colonies on the continent of Africa, Asia and in the West. These experiences while growing up in Jamaica, the impact of my colonial education, and my desire to "understand my roots," as we say in Jamaica, formed my lens of decolonization, and anti-colonial and anti-racist education. This desire to embrace my Blackness and disrupt the impact of colonial education led me to see education and schooling as sites of change and resistance. As a secondary school teacher and administrator in one of Canada's largest school boards further cemented my desire to engage in decolonizing praxis. Decolonial thinking is not new and existed since the inception of modern forms of colonization and is an unfinished project that is still unfolding (Maldonado-Torres, 2011). As a descendant of the enslaved, how I show up in spaces personally and professionally matter. I choose to show up grounded in the African knowledges of my ancestors and surrounded by their spirit. As Wane (2019) asserts:

> Indigenous knowledges are lived experiences and they are ways and systems of being and seeing. In these knowledges we ground our experiential

practices and our theoretical systems. In other words, African ways of knowing inform their practice and vice versa. (p. 13)

These knowledges are passed on through multiple generations (McGadney-
Douglass & Douglass, 2008).

EDUCATION AS A COLONIAL PROJECT

Settler colonialism invaded communities resulting in epistemic violence
on Indigenous and colonized people everywhere. This was done through
education by destroying the ways of knowing and culture of those they
colonized. The goal of colonizers and the colonizing enterprise was to
create homogenous understandings of social organizing practices built
around authority and leadership, and centered the knowledge of the colonizers (Prakash & Esteva, 2008). Garcia and Natividad (2018) note that
"even though education is touted as social mobility and freedom for
Indigenous peoples [including Indigenous peoples of Africa and other
colonized spaces], the politics of knowledge production and dissemination are ultimately tied to modern Western ordering of the world" (p. 28).

The manifestations of settler colonialism in education is the stripping
away from local communities their identities and forms of cultural initia-
tion (Prakash & Esteva, 2008). Educational policies have stripped students of their languages, promoted monolingualism, and positioned
multilingualism as a challenge (Crawford, 2000). Ngũgĩ wa Thiong'o
(1986), *Decolonising the Mind: The Politics of Language in African
Literature*, wrote about the systematic destruction of Kenyan tribal languages in schools. In Jamaica the local dialect "patois" was shunned, and
schools to educate girls and boys steeped in the knowledge of the colonizers were set up all across the island. These schools are still in operation
today with the history and knowledge of the colonizers revered in school
songs, school systems, and culture of schools.

The power of colonizing knowledge and the potential for taking hold
and moving through generations is evident in schooling practices and customs such as school songs and school names in the former colonies like
Jamaica. The current school song of a secondary school in Jamaica refer-
ences Dickenson and Munro and their effort to train the youth and sup-
posedly for which the colonized are grateful. "To educate demands great
care, so honour much the worthy pair, who gave their means and nobly
planned, to train the youths of this fair land" (Hamptonschool.edu, 2020).

This song goes on "so loudly let your praises flow to Dickenson and Hugh Munro" (Hamptonschool.edu, 2020).

The violence of colonialism is not only limited to occupation of land and resources, but extends to the occupation of mind and being (Bulhan, 2015). Garcia and Natividad (2018) suggest that the colonial project of education is also present in higher education, as evidenced by the lack of Indigenous and local customs and traditions at universities in the West, and they have been used as tools for acculturation. Institutions of higher education solidified coloniality of power and white supremacy, and we continue to see vestiges of this racial/colonial project as evidenced by an inequitable access to and graduation from postsecondary education for racially minoritized students (Dache-Gerbino, 2017, as cited in Garcia & Natividad, 2018).

The world is engulfed in turmoil as people who have been denied justice take to the streets to call for the dismantling of white supremacy, systemic racism and oppression, end to anti-Black racism, anti-Indigenous racism, and neoliberal policies that have marginalized and oppressed some groups and in particular Black, Indigenous, People of Color. Moments and movements capture the linkages between colonialism, racism, and other forms of dehumanization (Maldonado-Torres, 2011). This linkage has led to educators and people in all areas of social and political life to pursue decolonization in various spaces and contexts. Decolonizing education has been pursued in many forms by scholars, activists, and practitioners. In this book I trouble discourses and practices in educational leadership, and particularly school leadership, with a call to decolonization as a means of improving student outcomes and achievement.

The Covid-19 pandemic has laid bare structural inequities and systemic racism in education and all aspects of society and many are looking to leaders to guide this critical moment in time. Teaching, learning, and leading in schools must change if schools are to respond to the needs of BIPOC students. Research in many Western countries show that BIPOC students are not faring well in school, because of systemic racism, and discrimination at all levels. Research conducted by James and Turner (2017) with Black students from the Toronto District School Board—the largest school board in Canada—shows that Black students are not graduating at the same rate as others and are more likely to drop out. James and Turner (2017) data show that within cohort of students where data were collected:

84% of White students had graduated from high school at the end of 5 years, compared to 87% of other racialized students. By contrast, only 69% of their Black peers had graduated from high school over the same 5-year period. Similarly, Black students were twice as likely (11%) as White and other racialized students (both 5%) to be returning to high school the following year and twice as likely to have dropped out (20%) compared to White (11%) and other racialized students (9%). (p. 31)

There are similar statistics for Indigenous students. In 2018, the province wide graduation rate after five years of secondary education stood at 87% overall. For First Nations students, this rate was on only 60% (People for Education, 2018). These data show that schools rooted in colonial dominance in Ontario Canada, need to do a better job of supporting BIPOC students. This includes teachers, administrators, staff, and all those involved with students. The absence of decolonial educators and curriculum make schools unsafe spaces for some BIPOC students (Daniel, 2018). As Absolon (2019) argues marginalized people have common interests in decolonizing education.

Decolonization is a process that belongs to everyone (Bouvier, 2013). For decades Indigenous scholars in the West and the Global South have been advancing decolonizing theories and practices in education which seek to challenge racist and colonial ideologies and create space to build relationships grounded in shared understanding. Marie Battiste (2013), a Canadian Indigenous scholar and researcher, argues that decolonizing education is not a "process generated only for Indigenous students in the schools they attend or for students in First Nations programs in universities …but largely at the federal and provincial systems, the policy choices and inequities coming from them" (p. 14). The modern education system in Canada, Battiste (2013) argues, was created to maintain the identity; language, and culture of a colonial society, where culture is positioned as an educational concept that allowed Euro-Canadians to focus on empowering the powerless, while not having to confront the effects of racism or colonialism on the cultures of the 'other.' Decolonizing education calls for white supremacy, whiteness, and colonial systems of dominance to be dismantled.

CONCLUSION

This chapter situates this volume within the context of my research and ontological experiences. It sets out my personal, professional, and epistemological purpose for writing this volume. Reflecting on my positionality, experiences as a secondary school teacher, and experiences of the colonial education I received in Jamaica, has helped me to formulate the areas of focus for the rest of the book. The ideas posited are not a prescriptive but as a critical pedagogical exercise (Andreotti, Stein, Ahenakew, & Hunt, 2015) that acknowledges continued tensions in education and schooling. The challenge for educators is to be able to reflect critically on the current educational system in terms of whose knowledge is offered, who decides what is offered, what outcomes are rewarded, and who benefits (Battiste, 2008).

Decolonizing education allows "one to determine one's own site for decolonizing in terms of one's role, responsibilities, and duties in engaging in respectful relationships that do not replicate power and control dynamics of colonizer/colonized, confronts fear, assumptions, and false realities" (Absolon, 2019, p. 14). Building on my previous work in *Culturally Responsive Leadership and Socially Just Leadership* (Lopez, 2016), this book is intended to posit new frameworks within educational leadership discourse and practice, as a way to engage in conversations about what it means to intentionally challenge the vestiges of colonialism and neocolonialism in educational leadership. It is the hope that educators and practitioners of educational leadership will find this approach useful in improving the educational outcomes of students and in particular BIPOC students who are consistenlty marginalized by the education system. Decolonizing approaches to leadership is in contrast to Western models and frameworks that foreground hierarchies, bureaucracies, and neoliberal educational practices (Knaus & Brown, 2016). Drawing on Shultz (2012) I attempt to locate decolonizing educational praxis and education in ways that might help practitioners claim it for generative and regenerative work that will improve the lives of students who continue to learn in spaces dominated by Eurocentric ways of knowing while unsettling coloniality.

The following chapters complete this volume. They include examining educational leadership discourse challenges and possibilities, exploring how coloniality has informed educational leadership discourse. Decolonizing of the mind is suggested as process of unlearning, relearning, rereading, and reframing of the work of educational leaders. Capacities that educational and school leaders need to develop to implement decolonizing leadership are explored, and Chap. 6 examines ways that school leaders can engage in renewal of self and supporting others by creating space for recentering and reconnecting. The volume concludes with suggestions for moving forward for the field of educational leadership, scholars, and practitioners.

REFERENCES

Absolon, K. (2019). Indigenous wholistic theory: A knowledge set for practice. *First Peoples Child & Family Review, 14*(1), 22–42. Retrieved from https://fpcfr.com/index.php/FPCFR/article/view/370.

Andreotti, V., Stein, S., Ahenakew, C., & Hunt, D. (2015). Mapping interpretations of decolonization in the context of higher education. *Decolonization, Indigeneity, Education & Society, 4*(1), 22–40.

Battiste, M. (2008). The decolonization of Aboriginal education: Dialogue, reflection, and action in Canada. In P. R. Dasen & A. Akkari (Eds.), *Educational theories and practices ferom the majoroty world* (pp. 168–195). New Delhi: Sage Publishing.

Battiste, M. (2013). *Decolonizing education: Nourishing the learning spirit.* Saskatoon, SK: Purich Publishing.

Bouvier, R. (2013). Foreword. In M. Battiste (Ed.), *Decolonizing education: Nourishing the learning spirit* (pp. 8–12). Saskatoon, SK: Purich Publishing.

Bulhan, H. A. (2015). Stages of colonialism in Africa: From occupation of land to occupation of being. *Journal of Social and Political Psychology: Special Thematic Section on Decolonizing Psychology Science, 3*, 239–256.

Crawford, J. (2000). *At war with diversity: US language policy in an age of anxiety.* Clevedon: Multilingual Matters.

Dache-Gerbino, A. (2017). Mapping the postcolonial across urban and suburban college access geographies. *Equity & Excellence in Education, 50*(4), 368–386.

Daniel, B.-J. (2018). Knowing the self and the reason for being: Navigating racism in the academy. *Canadian Woman Studies/Les ca hiersde la femme, 32*(1–2), 59–66.

Garcia, G. A., & Natividad, N. D. (2018). Decolonizing leadership practices: Towards equity and justice at Hispanic-Serving institutions (HSIs)s and emerging HISs (eHSIs). *Journal of Transformative Leadership and Policy Studies, 7*(2), 25–39.

Hampton School. (2020). School song. Retrieved from http://hamptonschool.edu.jm/?page_id=150

James, C. E., & Turner, T. (2017). *Towards race equity in education: The schooling of Black students in the Greater Toronto Area.* Toronto, ON: York University.

Knaus, C. B., & Brown, M. C. (2016). *Whiteness in the new South Africa: Qualitative research on post-apartheid racism.* New York: Peter Lang.

Lopez, A. E. (2016). *Culturally responsive and socially just leadership: From theory to action.* New York: Palgrave Macmillan.

Maldonado-Torres, N. (2011). Thinking through the decolonial turn: Post-continental interventions in theory, philosophy, and critique—An introduction. *Transmodernity: Journal of Peripheral Cultural Production of the Luso-Hispanic World, 1*(2) Retrieved from https://escholarship.org/uc/item/59w8j02x.

McGadney-Douglass, B. F., & Douglass, R. L. (2008). Ghanaian mothers helping adult daughters: The survival of malnourished grandchildren. *Nana Araba Apt and Phyllis Antwi, 7*(2), 112–124.

People for Education. (2018). *Keeping up the momentun in Indigenous Education.* Retrieved fron https://peopleforeducation.ca/our-work/keeping-up-the-momentum-in-indigenous-education/.

Prakash, M., & Esteva, G. (2008). *Escaping education: Living as learning within grassroots cultures* (2nd ed.). New York: Peter Lang.

Shultz, L. (2012). Decolonizing social justice education: From policy knowledge to citizenship action. In A. A. Abdi (Ed.), *Decolonizing philosophies of education* (pp. 29–42). Rottterdam, Netherlands: Sense Publishers.

wa Thiong'o. (1986). *Decolonising the mind: The politics of language in African literature.* London: Portsmouth, N.H.: J. Curry; Heineman.

Wane, N. N. (2019). Is decolonizing the spirit possible? In N. N. Wane, M. Todorova, & K. Todd (Eds.), *Decolonizing the spirit in education and beyond.* Cham, Switzerland: Palgrave Macmillan.

CHAPTER 2

Examining Field of Educational Leadership: Challenges and Possibilities

Abstract This chapter examines educational leadership discourse, with a focus on school leadership. A brief overview of the history and evolution of the field of educational administration is explored. The dominance of Eurocentric knowledge and White bodies in the field, the lack of research, and discourse from the Global South are interrogated. The possibilities that decolonizing theorizing and practices offer the field of educational leadership and school leaders as a way of increasing the educational outcomes for BIPOC students are explored. Decolonizing educational praxis as a support for practitioners as generative and regenerative work is highlighted.

Keywords Educational leadership • School leadership • Decolonizing educational praxis • Colonial education

INTRODUCTION

While there continues to be contestations on the meaning of leadership, many insist that leadership as a construct is inherently good and urgently needed (Liu, 2020). Educational leadership is seen as an important factor in improving student outcomes and has become a priority for policy makers and researchers globally. Next to teaching, leadership is seen as an important factor in student achievement and learning (Leithwood,

© The Author(s), under exclusive license to Springer Nature Switzerland AG 2020
A. E. Lopez, *Decolonizing Educational Leadership*,
https://doi.org/10.1007/978-3-030-62380-7_2

Seashore-Louis, Anderson, & Wahlstrom, 2004). How leaders understand their roles and the frameworks that guide their thinking and practice is important if schools are to respond effectively to sociocultural shifts, and the demands of BIPOC students who are not thriving as they should, not achieving their full potential, and are pushed out of school due to systemic racism and other forms of oppression.

The field of educational leadership has been examined in order to understand and identify the kinds of leadership knowledge, skills, and practices to facilitate the achievement of desired student outcomes (Witziers, Bosker, & Kruger, 2003). Leadership has always been wrapped up in systems of power and often reinforces ideologies and practices of the status quo; and since sociologist Max Weber posited the notion of charismatic authority in the 1920s, leadership has engaged in enduring romance with great men who are believed to be vital to the success of organizations and societies (Liu, 2020). The dominance of white bodies in leadership roles is a lasting feature of colonialism that is evident in educational leadership and school leadership. Protests continue in Canada and across the Western world by Black Indigenous and People of Color (BIPOC) against anti-Black racism, anti-Indigenous racism, and other forms of oppression. Educators and community members are calling for greater equity, representation, and change in polices in leadership and other aspects of education. Critical educators argue that current leadership frameworks are inadequate to respond to these demands and alternative approaches must be found.

Western frameworks of educational leadership over the years have ignored alternative epistemologies in the study and practice of educational leadership (Hallinger & Leithwood, 1998; Dimmock & Walker, 2000). Education systems built on colonial structures continue to deny people of African descent, Indigenous peoples, and other racialized groups around the globe the opportunity to engage in education grounded in their epistemologies and histories (Lopez & Rugano, 2018). Under the impact of colonialism, neoliberalism, and globalization education continues to produce a system in which student disengagement, and inequities continue to thrive (McMahon & Portelli, 2004). This is evident in the challenge that Indigenous people in Canada and other Western countries, Black, and Brown people continue to face in education. Battiste (2008) argues that Eurocentric education and political systems and their assimilation processes have severely eroded and damaged Indigenous knowledge.

Conceptualization of educational leadership varies broadly, but generally considered to be leadership roles, within the larger context of education including K-12 schools and higher education. In higher education, educational leaders are often seen as people who hold formal leadership positions, such as deans, department chairs, president, provost, vice provost, directors of units such as student services, chief accounting officers, and others who influence academic policies, strategies, structures, management, resource allocation, and decision-making (Bolden, Petrov, & Gosling, 2009). School leadership is an aspect of educational leadership focused on K-12 schools. However, there are different understandings, concepts, and representations of school leadership which vary according to language, country, culture, and the structures that govern education (Pont, 2020). In this book school leadership refers to educators who have leading roles in K-12 schools. By leading roles, I mean those in administrative positions such as principals and vice principals and educators in non-administrative roles who also have an impact on student learning such as guidance counselors, instructional coaches, curriculum leads, and so forth.

School leadership has gained prominence in educational leadership discourse and research as evidence show that school leaders, next to teaching, have the greatest influence on student outcomes (see Leithwood et al., 2004). School leadership can also be spread across groups of people or teams, hence the term 'school leadership teams.' The uses of the term "school leadership" reflect changes in the role of leaders over the last twenty to thirty years (Pont, 2020). In many countries, a shift can be observed in their education systems towards a deeper involvement and collaborating with other teachers and staff for the improvement of school results more (Adams & Gaetane, 2011; Spillane & Kenney, 2012). This volume is primarily about leading and leadership in K-12 schools. While I have held leadership roles in higher education such as Academic Director of Initial Teacher Education, and currently the Director of the Center for Leadership and Diversity, and my role as Provostial Adviosr Access Programs much of my educational and leadership journey has been in K-12 schools, which are also the sites of my research. As a former secondary school teacher and administrator, I am deeply concerned about the impact of the schooling experiences on Black, Indigenous, and People of Color (BIPOC) students. School leaders are at the core of the processes of change in schools (Viennet & Pont, 2017) and should quite rightly be the focus of attention if coloniality in schools is to be disrupted and dismantled and the process of decolonization takes hold.

Historically educational leadership theory and practice has been normalized within Western Eurocentric understandings of leadership. Critical scholars and researchers continue to work toward the disruption of this reality and offer alternative approaches to leadership theorizing and practice, for example, culturally responsive leadership (Beachum, 2011; Lopez, 2016), social justice leadership (Bogotch & Reyes-Guerra, 2014; Theoharis, 2007), and transformative leadership (Shields, 2010). Notwithstanding these approaches, critical scholars agree that more educational research from the Global South and emerging economies are needed to broaden the field. The term 'Global South' is used for regions outside of Europe and North America, including Africa, Asia, Latin America, and Oceania characterized by emerging economies. Because of the importance of educational leadership to student outcomes, this kind of reimagining continues as scholars examine the kinds of leadership knowledge, skills, and practices that will improve student achievement, especially students who have traditionally been underserved in education systems. These students are usually Black, Indigenous, People of Color and live in poverty, particularly in countries that have experienced colonization (Hohepa, 2013). The current Canadian educational systems, which give preference to Eurocentric thinking, are not supporting Indigenous students as well as their non-Indigenous counterparts (Battiste, 2013). Decolonization of the existing model of education is imperative and educational leadership is crucial in this change. Educational leaders must be agentive in their thinking toward Indigenous peoples and model this thinking for others (Berryman, Carr-Stewart, Kovach, & Steeves, 2014).

Colonial remnants and sludge continue to be present in the discourses and practices of education policy and organization of schools. This is evident in the prevalence and dominance of white bodies in educational spaces, disciplinary practices, hierarchical organizational structures, prioritization of knowledge from bureaucrats instead of communities, the lack of inclusion in the teaching and learning process of knowledge grounded in the histories of students, are all remnants of colonial administrative practices (Bray & Koo, 2004). The legacy of colonialism is also reflected in the continued presence of structural racism and white supremacy in school leadership policies and practices. In my own experiences of schooling in Jamaica I learned nothing about my ancestors who were forcibly taken from the continent of Africa, their greatness, their contributions to civilization, science, math, language, astrology, trade, and other areas. What little was shared was of the essentialized "African" with a spear and loin cloth reinforcing their supposed "primitiveness." They were rendered as without knowledge, positioned as laborers, "lazy" when they challenged their oppressors. The continent reduced in size, diversity of its people diminished, and the resources up for the taking by colonial powers. Much of this positioning of Black people and people of African descent persists today, the result of which is the denial of our humanity and sometimes death at the hand of state and others.

Education systems across the world were introduced as part of imperialistic and colonizing practices which had a profound effect on those who were colonized, Indigenous epistemologies, values, beliefs, and practices (Grande, 2000). Schooling has historically been a site of colonization and assimilation, as a contemporary site of language and cultural regeneration and transmission (Penetito, 2010). Scholars such as Dei (2000), Grande (2004), and Smith (1999) contend that there are multiple incarnations of colonialism in the contemporary contexts of education and schooling tied to particular epistemology of control. Scholars such as Battiste (2013) call for decolonizing of the entire education system to fight against imperialism and racism. Abdi (2012) contends:

> colonialism in its psychological, educational, cultural, technological, economic and political dimensions has not been cleansed from all of its former colonies and colonized spaces. So much so that in schooling and attached social development platforms, the way of the colonial is not only still intact, it actually assumes the point of prominence in almost all transactions that affect the lives of people. (p. 2)

Colonial education in spaces that were colonized, for example, in the African context assured not only the supremacy of European languages and epistemologies, but the inferiorization of African worldviews, epistemic locations, styles of expression, and forms of description (Abdi, 2012; Achebe, 2000; wa Thiong'o, 1986). Abdi (2007) argues that knowledge, learning traditions, or oral societies were seen as backward, ineffective, and unacceptable in the new modalities of colonial relationships. This can still be seen in schools today. For example, how students from Jamaica, who speak the Jamaican dialect "patois" and enter schools in Canada, are made to feel uncomfortable about their way and manner of speaking and their knowledge undervalued.

BRIEF HISTORY OF EDUCATIONAL ADMINISTRATION
AND LEADERSHIP

Educational leadership or educational administration as it was known early on as a field of study emerged in the United States in the early twentieth century. Leadership in education became defined as "extracting the maximum efficiency from educational resources, both physical and human …this business-managerial conception of educational leadership dominated the emerging university-based programs of training in educational administration" (Bates, 2010, p. 724). Bates argues further that this approach to educational leadership reformed education from the top down through university programs and national organizations, "resulted in widespread transformation of leadership in American education and imposed the efficiencies of scientific management upon teachers, entrenched central administration control over curriculum and assessment; and replaced educational ideals with managerial goals" (p. 724). Centers were created at universities including the Ontario Institute for Studies in Education (OISE) in Canada charged with developing educational administrators, producing literature on educational administration, and supporting the establishment of professional organizations committed to this approach to educational administration (Moore, 1964). The effect was to embed systems theory and behavioral science as the theoretical foundations of educational administration and leadership (Bates, 2010). Over the years there has been a shift in emphasis from administration to leadership which has become the dominant theme (Bates, 2010).

The field was dominated by white men, who conducted much of the research within predominantly white contexts (Hallinger, 2019). This approach to educational leadership excluded the knowledge and voices of women, Black, Indigenous, and Racialized scholars, research from the Global South, and emerging economies from educational leadership research and discourse. Fitzgerald (2006) argues that the field of educational leadership still remains predominantly heteronormative, nonspiritual, middle-class, white, and masculine which produces hegemonic epistemologies. This has led to troubling problems and deficiencies in the field that persists till today (Brooks & Normore, 2018; Murphy, 2006).

Educational leadership research and practice continue to focus on schools and as such school leadership has taken on greater significance in educational leadership discourse. Schools remain sites of oppression for many students and the furtherance of colonial legacies.

School leadership theorizing, policies, and practice that disrupt colonial legacies in education are important to achieving better educational outcomes for students. The conversation in this book is about schools and those in positions of leadership both in formal and informal spaces. Leadership is constructed to include those in administrative positions such as principals and vice principals, and those who impact student learning outcomes, school culture, and organization, such as resource teachers, instructional coaches, and curriculum leaders. These roles vary depending on context.

There is a paucity of approaches within educational leadership discourse that highlight the ongoing presence of coloniality and foregrounds decolonizing frameworks. Indigenous scholars such as Battiste (2013), Hohepa (2013), Penetito (2010), Smith (1999), and others argue for decolonizing approaches in education that seek to affirm the value of Indigenous and former colonized people, protect, support, and grow leadership, in order that it can help to make a positive difference to student outcomes (Hohepa, 2013). I contend in this book that the ways in which educational leadership, and by extension school leadership, is practiced are steeped in colonial impositions and ideologies and must be disrupted.

Decolonizing Educational Leadership

Attempts to decolonize education and actively resist colonial paradigms is a complex and daunting task (Battiste, 2008). Decolonization means removing vestiges of colonialism from all aspects of schooling and education. Even though I focus on educational leadership in this volume, I am mindful that it is not enough to decolonize one part of the teaching, learning, and leading process and that teaching and learning must also be decolonized. There are scholars who have posited notions and ideas on decolonizing the curriculum, assessment and other aspects of teaching and learning. Colonization and its lasting effects and its means of control have been perpetuated through educational and leadership practices over the years.

The aim of this volume is to critically examine educational leadership and reimagine how school leadership policies and practices can intentionally name and disrupt colonial remnants in discourses and practices of education policy and organization of schools. Toward this goal the book is grounded decolonizing discourses that seek to reposition educational leadership in a way that reconstruct systems that affirm the identities as well as the existentialities of students (Abdi, 2012). Decolonizing approaches create space for students and educators to draw on their histories, anchor themselves in their stories, and use this knowledge for their educational advancement, and by doing so disrupt the colonial project of schooling that seeks to erase the knowledge of Black, Indigenous, and People of Color (BIPOC), and police and control them. Schooling and education have been seen by some oppressed people as a way of improving their economic and social position in society. For many this educational pursuit has inflicted violence and harm as schools which are historically sites of colonization thwart their educational efforts and desires.

CONCLUSION

In this chapter I have provided an overview of educational and school leadership discourse and the emergence of the field over time. Knowledge base of the field and arguments for grounding of leadership theorizing and practices in decolonizing perspective are examined. The urgency and need for changes in leadership approaches and practice is clear. Educators must seek to hasten what Abdi (2012) refers to as "incomplete processes of epistemic decolonization" (p. 2) by positing alternative ways of theorizing and engaging in leadership practice (Patel, 2015). Educators need to make intentional decisions to disrupt Eurocentric epistemes, change practices, and embrace decolonizing approaches to teaching, learning, and leading. They must be able to identify the practices and what it means to lead in ways that are decolonizing and empowering to themselves and their students.

REFERENCES

Abdi, A. (Ed.). (2012). *Decolonizing philosophies of education.* Rotterdam, Netherlands: Sense Publishers.

Abdi, A. A. (2007). Oral societies and colonial experiences: Sub-Saharan Africa, and the de-facto power of the written word. *International Education, 37*(1), 42–59.

Achebe, C. (2000). *Home and exile.* New York: Oxford University Press.

Adams, C., & Gaetane, J. (2011). A diffusion approach to study leadership reform. *Journal of Educational Administration, 49*(4), 354– 377.

Bates, R. (2010). History of educational leadership/management. In P. Peterson, E. Baker, & B. Mcgraw (Eds.), *International encyclopedia of education* (pp. 724–730). Elsevier Ltd.

Battiste, M. (2008). Research ethics for protecting Indigenous knowledge and heritage: Institutional and researcher responsibilities. In N. Denzin, Y. S. Lincoln, & L. Tuhawi Smith (Eds.), *Handbook of critical and Indigenous methodologies* (pp. 497–509). Los Angeles, CA: Sage.

Battiste, M. (2013). *Decolonizing education: Nourishing the learning spirit.* Saskatoon, SK: Purich Publishing.

Beachum, F. (2011). Culturally relevant leadership for complex 21st century school contexts. In F. English (Ed.), *The Sage handbook of educational leadership* (4th ed., pp. 27–35). Thousand Oaks, CA: Sage Publications.

Berryman, M., Carr-Stewart, S. B., Kovach, M., & Steeves, L. E. (2014). *Seeking their voices: Improving indigenous student learning outcomes.* Regina, SK: Saskatchewan Instructional Development and Research Unit.

Bogotch, I., & Reyes-Guerra, D. (2014). Leadership for social justice: Social pedagogies. *Revista Internacional de Educacion para la Justicia Social, 3*(2), 33–58.

Bolden, R., Petro, G., & Gosling, J. (2009). Distributed leadership in higher education: Rhetoric and reality. *Education Management Administration & Leadership, 37*(2), 257–277.

Bray, M., & Koo, R. (2004). Postcolonial patterns and paradoxes: Language and education in Honk Kong and Macao. *Comparative Education, 40,* 215–239.

Brooks, J. S., & Normore, A. H. (2018). *Leading against the Grain: Lessons from visionaries for creating just and equitable schools.* New York: Teachers College Press.

Dei, G. S. (2000). Rethinking the role of indigenous knowledges in the academy. *International Journal of Inclusive Education, 4*(2), 111–132.

Dimmock, C., & Walker, A. (2000). Developing comparative and international educational leadership and management: A cross-cultural model. *School Leadership and Management, 20*(2), 143–160.

Fitzgerald, T. (2006). Walking between two worlds: Indigenous women and educational leadership. *Educational Management Administration & Leadership, 34*(2), 201–213.

Grande, S. (2000). American Indian geographies of identity and power: At the crossroads of Indigenous and Mestizaje. *Harvard Educational Review, 70*(4), 467–498.

Grande, S. (2004). *Red pedagogy: Native American social and political thought.* Lanham, NJ: Rowan & Littlefield.

Hallinger, P. (2019). Science mapping the knowledge base on educational leadership and management from the emerging regions of Asia, Africa, and Latin America, 1965–2018. *Educational Management Administration & Leadership, 48*(2), 11–32.

Hallinger, P., & Leithwood, K. (1998). Unseen forces: The impact of social culture on school leadership. *Peabody Journal of Education, 73,* 126–151.

Hohepa, M. K. (2013). Educational leadership and indigeneity: Doing things the same. *American Journal of Education, 119*(4), 617–631.

Leithwood, K., Seashore-Louis, K. S., Anderson, S., & Wahlstrom, K. (2004). *How leadership influences student learning: Review of research.* New York: Wallace Foundation.

Liu, H. (2020). *In Redeeming leadership: An anti-racist and feminist intervention.* Bristol: Bristol University Press.

Lopez, A. E. (2016). *Culturally responsive and socially just leadership: From theory to action.* New York: Palgrave Macmillan.

Lopez, A. E., & Rugano, P. (2018). Educational leadership in Post-Colonial Kenya: What can we learn from the experiences of three female principals in Kenyan secondary schools? *Education Sciences, 8*(99), 1–15.

McMahon, B., & Portelli, J. P. (2004). Engagement for what? Beyond popular discourses of student engagement. *Leadership and Policy in Schools, 3*(1), 59–76.

Moore, H. A. (1964). The ferment in school administration. In D. E. Griffiths (Ed.), *Behavioural science and educational administration* (pp. 11–32). NSSE Yearbook.

Murphy, J. (2006). *Preparing school leaders: Defining a research and action agenda.* Lanham, MD: Rowman & Littlefield Education.

Patel, L. (2015). *Decolonizing educational research: From ownership to answerability.* New York: Routledge.

Penetito, W. (2010). *What's Maori, about Maori education.* Wellington: Victoria University Press.

Pont, B. (2020). A literature review of school leadership policy reforms. *European Journal of Education, 55,* 154–168. Retrieved from https://doi.org/10.1111/ejed.12398.

Shields, C. M. (2010). Transformative leadership: Working for equity in diverse contexts. *Educational Administration Quarterly, 46*(4), 558–589.

Smith, L. T. (1999). *Decolonizing methodologies: Research and Indigenous peoples.* London: Zed Books.

Spillane, J., & Kenney, A. (2012). School administration in a changing education sector: The US experience. *Journal of Educational Administration, 50*(5), 541–561.

Theoharis, G. (2007). Social justice educational leaders and resistance: Toward a theory of social justice leadership. *Educational Administration Quarterly, 43*(2), 221–258.

Viennet, R., & Pont, B. (2017). Education policy implementation: A literature review and proposed framework. *OECD Working Paper,* No. 162 https://doi.org/10.1177/0013161X03253411.

wa Thiong'o, N. (1986). *Decolonizing the mind: The politics of language in African literature.* London: James Curry.

Witziers, B., Bosker, R., & Kruger, M. (2003). Educational leadership and student achievement: The elusive search for an association. *Educational Administration Quarterly, 39*(3), 398–425.

CHAPTER 3

Coloniality and Educational Leadership Discourse

Abstract This chapter examines the notion of coloniality within anti-colonial discourse. It explores the convergences and divergences with other ways of theorizing impact of colonialism and coloniality. It examines ways that scholars and practitioners can engage in anti-colonial praxis. Coloniality of power and knowledge is examined through the work of Aníbal Quijano—a Latin American scholar. The chapter concludes by exploring how coloniality gains power and connections to the day-to-day realities of education and schooling.

Keywords Anti-colonial • Coloniality • Coloniality of power • Coloniality of knowledge • Decolonizing philosophy

Introduction

Decolonization is the process of undoing coloniality (Oyedemi, 2020). Placing coloniality within education leadership discourse allows educational leaders to examine their practices through alternative epistemic lens. Coloniality is not a topic that is often seen in educational and school leadership discourse. In this volume I am suggesting that educational leaders who undergird their practice through decolonizing frameworks should engage with notions of coloniality as a starting point, since decolonization in essence is the undoing and dismantling of coloniality. Coloniality is not

A. E. Lopez, *Decolonizing Educational Leadership*,
https://doi.org/10.1007/978-3-030-62380-7_3

21

the same as colonialism. While colonialism is a method of governing and control by some countries, coloniality is ongoing through systems such as white supremacy and racism. Coloniality persists in education through its reliance on Eurocentric logic and ways of knowing and organizational practices at all levels of education and schooling at the expense of subaltern epistemologies.

Eurocentric knowledge acts as a kind of distorting mirror that makes people believe what they are not, what they never should have been, and what they never will be. This distorts reality and the real problems, and thwarts workable solutions except only in partial and distorted way (Quijano, 2000). Conversations on coloniality brings voices especially from the Global South that are sparse in educational research and discourse. The history of educational leadership and educational administration as a white male-dominated area field of study makes the field a space where coloniality lingers. Disrupting coloniality in educational leadership creates space for other epistemological and ontological theorizing and practices and builds on other critical discourse and frameworks such as culturally responsive leadership, social justice leadership, and transformative leadership.

Coloniality refers to long-standing patterns of power that emerged as a result of colonialism, but that define culture, labor, intersubjective relations, and knowledge production well beyond the strict limits of colonial administrations. It is maintained through books, standards for academic performance, cultural patterns, the self-image of peoples, aspirations of self, and many other aspects of our modern experience. As modern subjects we engage with coloniality all the time and everyday (Maldonado-Torres, 2007). Coloniality must be named to be countered in order for material change to occur. Decolonization requires the apprehension and unsettling of coloniality (Tuck & Yang, 2012). Coloniality in its many forms includes exercise of power and control of knowledge as well as produces racialized hierarchies and erasures (Tucker, 2018).

SITUATING COLONIALITY WITHIN ANTI-COLONIAL DISCOURSE

An understanding of coloniality provides a framework to engage in decolonial and decolonizing work. While some scholars point to some distinctions between decolonial work and decolonizing work, both seek to disrupt imperialist and colonizing practices, past and present (Mendoza, 2015). Situating decolonial theory within the broader body of philosophical anti-colonial work positions it against systems of colonial oppression (Velez & Tuana, 2020). Nonetheless, Velez and Tuana (2020) warn of creating binaries and the importance of affirming differences among schools of thought. They note:

> In order to affirm differences among schools of thought in anticolonial philosophy, we further distinguish between decolonial thinking emerging from distinct geopolitical locations and histories of struggles against colonization: for example, Africana contexts, Black American contexts, Caribbean contexts, Indigenous contexts, Latin American contexts, and U.S. Latinx contexts. Though these strands of decolonial thought mutually influence and complement each other, they are not coterminous or exhaustive of one another nor are they in and of themselves internally cohesive or noncontradictory. This is, in part, due to diverse responses to multiplicitous forms and experiences of current and ongoing practices of colonization. These practices are found in settler-colonial contexts such as the United States, as well as in the continued and lasting imprint of past forms of colonization that Quijano has described as coloniality. Indeed, each form of decolonial thinking offers its own distinct contributions to anticolonial philosophy as it outlines and prioritizes different sets of decolonial imperatives (pp. 3–4).

Decolonial theorizing as part of the larger project of anti-colonial thought, has different roots that span geographical and cultural contexts. A decolonial lens highlights the history of colonization particular to the Americas that is often occluded in postcolonial theories, which tends to focus on the impact of European colonial rule (Velez & Tuana, 2020). Together and collectively these theories offer ways of thinking about the impact colonization, deepen insights, inform research and practice. As Majumdar (2017) argues, postcolonial theory provides a framework for understanding how power works in modern social constructions and in particular how the West exercises its continued dominance over the Global South.

While Velez and Tuana's (2020) work focuses on what they refer to as "decolonial feminism," they urge scholars to nurture the complexity and differences among different ways of philosophizing experiences that arise from our locations and positionalities as this allows us to examine the "importance of theorizing from within transgressive and subaltern imaginaries for the task of thinking beyond and outside of the delimited arena of the dominant symbolic order" (p. 13). Velez and Tuana (2020) suggest that transgressive and subaltern imaginaries are necessary conditions for developing new liberatory rhythms and possibilities in thinking and praxis. Perez refers to this "the decolonial imaginary" which is an aggregation of histories, experiences, and images, that operate like a rich, critical machinery for recovering voices and experiences of the oppressed. Decolonial imaginary presents a transgressive space-time through which decolonizing gestures find purpose. Velez and Tuana (2020) argue that when this imaginary is emphasized new approaches and ways of thinking emerge that shed light on "structures, practices, and images in which social imaginaries are implicated in the processes of colonization and how theorizing from alternative imaginaries opens up new possibilities for resistance and liberation" (p. 13).

The 'colonial' still exists (Simmons & Dei, 2012) which necessitates critical scholars finding space to continue work of disruption, in all aspects of social and political life including schooling. Anti-colonial frameworks offer such possibilities. In examining how anti-colonial frameworks can support this work of understanding the "operations of colonial and re-colonial relations and the implications," Simmons and Dei (2012) suggest the following notions. I draw on this framing to explicate as it connects theory to practice and advances ways that educators can begin this kind of praxis and engage.

1. Understanding processes of knowledge production, Indigenity, and local Indigenousness, and the pursuit of agency, resistance, and subjective politics.
2. Recognize that all knowledge must purposively serve to challenge colonial imposition.
3. 'Colonial' is understood in the sense of not simply 'foreign or alien,' but more profoundly as 'imposed and dominating.'
4. Colonialism is read as an imposition and domination that never ended with the return of political sovereignty to colonized peoples or nation states or independence.
5. Theorize the nature and extent of social domination, and, particularly, the multiple places of power and how these relations of power work to establish dominant-subordinate connections.
6. Engaging with concepts as colonialism, oppression, colonial encounter, decolonization, power, agency, and resistance, and claiming the authenticity of local voice and intellectual agency of peoples.

7. Create space for an integrated and intersectional analysis of colonialism, imperialism, and decolonization.
8. Recognize the central place of spirituality and the spiritual knowing.
9. The saliency of Indigenity (as identity) and the Indigene (in terms of the authenticity of voice) anchored in the Indigenous sense of collective and common colonial consciousness. Knowledge that emerges from the "ground-up" in terms of local peoples understanding their experiences in the context of colonialism, colonial, and re-colonial relations and other associated oppressions.
10. Articulate the connections between colonialism, oppression, and change.
11. The dominant must be prepared to invoke and act on their complicities and responsibilities through a politics of accountability.
12. Important to bring a trans-historical analysis to the understanding of colonial privilege that challenges and subverts the implication of the 'post' in postcolonialism. Signals that the implications of colonialism are ongoing.

Simmons and Dei (2012) suggest understanding the "colonial as anything imposed and dominating, allows the anti-colonial discursive framework to engage the intersections of race, ethnicity, class, gender, disability, sexuality, linguistic, and religion-based oppressions through historical moments across time and space as sites of power and resistance" (p. 79). This is imporant as people experience oppression through multiple and intersecting points of their identitites.

Coloniality of Knowledge and Power

Drawing on the work of Quijano (2000, 2007), a Peruvian sociologist, I explore notions of coloniality as a base of understanding to engage in decolonizing and decolonial praxis. The colonial period according to Quijano (2007) was marked by patterns of repression, expropriation, and imposition of knowledge refracted through ideas of race and racial hierarchy. This foregrounded a "particular set of global material relations and intersubjectivities and a colonial model of global power characterized by continued racialization and racial hierarchization, the concentration of resources, trade and economic production in Western Europe and North America, and the dominance of a particular form of Eurocentric knowledge" (Quijano 2000, pp. 537–542). Quijano (2000) named this model of control and suppression, which he suggests is still central to global political, economic, and epistemic relations, as "coloniality." Quijano suggests that Eurocentric knowledge that dominates education and all aspects of life is a "specific rationality or perspective of knowledge that was made globally hegemonic" through the interconnected workings of colonialism and capitalism (Quijano, 2000, pp. 549–550). Quijano (2000) described coloniality as manifesting in at least three interconnected and interdependent forms:

- *Systems of hierarchies*: racial division and classification as the organizing principle of White supremacy
- *Systems of knowledge*: privileging of Western or Eurocentric forms of knowledge as universal and objective
- *Societal systems*: reinforcing hierarchies through construction of the state and specific institutions to regulate, segregate, and diminish decolonizing systems of healing and lived experiences

Coloniality of power, as Quijano (2000) describes it, maintains the political and economic spheres of colonialism that are linked to white supremacy and power. Quijano suggests that coloniality of power was used in, for example, the United States to advance racial hierarchies, positioning some who are considered worthy of being close to whiteness, others at the bottom and the laboring class, using this to control labor and develop global power around capitalist-wage labor relations. Garcia and Natividad (2018) argue "that power relations that developed during colonization of the Americas shaped the development of racial and economic epistemic structures of power that are evidenced and (re)nscribed in numerous institutions" (p. 27). This includes the commodification of education that is linked to defining and reinforcing identities that separate people into the dominant and the oppressed, which results in "division of labor and the idea of race as structurally and mutually reinforcing" (p. 28). Tucker (2018) suggests that coloniality sets up Western European knowledgea and practices as timeless, while rendering Indigenous knowledges as something associated with the past. This positioning gives primacy to Eurocentric knowledge. Tucker argues:

> "Coloniality of knowledge" refers to historically rooted, racially inflected practices that routinely elevate the knowledge forms and knowledge-generating principles of colonizing cultures, whilst relegating those of colonized cultures. It draws attention to the constitutive role of knowledge in the violences that characterized colonial domination and to the role of

knowledge in perpetuating the patterns of racial hierarchization and oppression that were established … It also reflects the hierarchical, temporal logics of what Quijano calls "Eurocentric knowledge," such that Western European knowledges and practices appear timeless, while the knowledges and practices of indigenous peoples are associated with the past (p. 220).

Quijano (2000) suggests that colonial domination relies on the idea of race as a means of classifying and hierarchizing populations. In the periods of occupation colonial repression was cemented through "modes of knowing, of producing knowledge, of producing perspectives, images and systems of images, symbols, modes of signification" of colonized cultures, as well as of their "resources, patterns, and instruments of formalised and objectivized expression" (Quijano, 2007, p. 169).

Coloniality is built on inequitable power and hierarchies of knowledge. This structure must be dismantled, and epistemic privileges of coloniality removed (Mignolo, 2009). To be decolonial is to embrace epistemic discomfort of dislodging coloniality through ontological distance, and center the ontological and epistemic experiences of the subaltern and historically marginalized communities and youths in schools. The realities of colonial historicity, with its painful and visceral truths, tell us about the nature and deployment of power in and across social, cultural, and racial difference (Okihiro, 2014). Through meaningful consideration of epistemic perspectives on liberation, power, and knowledge that emerges from the historically marginalized communities and experiences, will emerge authentic appreciation of the knowledge and brilliance of subaltern communities. This can only be achieved by ontological distance from coloniality (Domínguez, 2019). I am not suggesting that this will be an easy task for educational leaders, but it is a necessary and important one. Keeping ontological distance means that educators must decenter whiteness in schooling practices, and the experiences of those who have been traditionally excluded and marginalized centred in discourse and practice. It means in practice that BIPOC educators must be in positions of leadership bringing their experiences and knowledge to the decision-making table.

Developing Decolonizing Philosophy

Intellectuals seeking to advance the discourse of decolonization must be aware of epistemic decolonization that builds new concepts, theories, and ideas (Maldonado-Torres, 2011). It is important to signal that there are complexities to any discussion about coloniality which are beyond the scope of this book. De L'Estolle (2008) suggests there is a proliferation of coloniality discourses, but there is little detailed discussion of the concrete forms that colonial oppressions and struggles have taken around the world. There is not enough effort to specify and unpack the diverse elements and mechanisms that contribute to colonial patterns of racialized hierarchization and oppression (Tucker, 2018). As we examine the pervasiveness of coloniality in all aspects of life and education, Patel (2014) suggests that everyone is implicated through its ongoing structure of people, land, and well-being. Patel (2014) argues that:

> Coloniality, because of its pervasiveness, implicates everyone through its ongoing structure of people, land, and well-being. These implications do not mean that anyone's social location relative to colonization is fixed by virtue of birthplace or social identity, but rather at every juncture there is constant opportunity and responsibility to identify and counter the genealogies of coloniality that continue to require oppression (p. 358).

As we encourage educators to engage in decolonizing education it is important to warn as Tuck and Yang (2012) have advocated, that the process of colonization is not over and decolonization must not be used as a metaphor. Coloniality has kept stable the core project of material domination, whether through religious or state-defined delineations of worth or other forms (Patel, 2014). Some scholars argue for an "anti-colonial" and "decolonial" discursive framework to signal that the struggle against coloniality is ongoing. Patel (2014) suggests that her use of the term "anti-colonial" is a pause from the overuse of the term decolonization, with the intention of better leveraging both terms. Patel (2014) posits that anti-colonial still allows for "locating the hydra-like shape-shifting yet implacable logics of settler colonialism, but does not include in its semantic shape the unmet promises of stripping away colonization, as the term *decolonization* gestures tend to do. This, in itself, marks anticolonial stances as incomplete" (p. 361). While this book is grounded in a decolonizing framework, school leaders and others engaging in decolonizing education are encouraged to keep in mind that decolonization is a process, and makes revisiting current research and emerging literature part of ongoing practice.

It is important for educational leaders to develop a decolonizing philosophy that guides action. All educators at some point on their educational journey have had to write out their philosophy of education or teaching. This usually takes the form of writing what one thinks about education, exploring such ideas as the purpose education should serve, and sometimes provide examples to support the notions being advocated. Each person who writes out a philosophy of education might have a different approach to discussing their philosophy or have a different understanding of educational issues. Regardless of the diversity in educators' philosophical dispositions, what educators think and believe about education, students, learning, and school leadership their philosophy guide practice and the decisions that are made.

Abdi (2012) suggests that philosophies of education focus on the rationale as well as the reasonableness of learning programs and are specific to historical and geographical locations and calls out what he sees as the de-philosophization of colonized populations built on the notion that they are not capable of higher level thinking. This positioning of colonized and marginalized peoples as lacking in thought and ideas, and therefore must be guided by dominant ideologies, misrepresents the long histories that have informed cultures and practices before the colonizers arrived. Abdi (2012) contends that in the "most contemporary, so-called postcolonial spaces of education and schooling, the native elite has failed in deconstructing colonial philosophies and epistemologies of education … a decolonizing philosophy of education that leads to decolonized platforms of learning, should also instigate decolonized platforms of development" (p. 5). Abdi deliberately connects the philosophical and the epistemological to show how dominant and hegemonic philosophies translate into worldviews and knowledge that govern the lives of people, learning systems in education, and other aspects of society.

Engagement in decolonizing education requires educators to actively counter these narratives. In these efforts Abdi (2012) suggests that educators "counter the descriptive and analytical levels which are initially responsible for the formative stages of the philosophical and the epistemological, the continuities of coloniality based education and attached ways of reading and relating to the world … and that it is important to establish a body of anticolonial criticisms and deconstructionist notations that hasten the now incomplete processes of epistemic decolonization, which could slowly liberate spaces and intersections of learning and social progress" (p. 6).

The task of decolonization is not easy and should not be trivialized. Attaching of the word decolonization to practices in schools, assessment, curriculum, leadership, pedagogy without a sound understanding of the impact of coloniality, colonialism, neocolonialism, historical roots, and contemporary manifestations can do more harm than good. Tuck and Yang (2012) warn:

> decolonization is not a metaphor. When metaphor invades decolonization, it kills the very possibility of decolonization; it recenters whiteness, it resettles theory, it extends innocence to the settler, it entertains a settler future. Decolonize (a verb) and decolonization (a noun) cannot easily be grafted onto pre-existing discourses/frameworks, even if they are critical, even if they are anti-racist, even if they are justice frameworks. The easy absorption, adoption, and transposing of decolonization is yet another form of settler appropriation (p. 3).

Fanon (1963) argues that decolonization is a historical process, which sets out to change the order of the world, is, obviously, a program of complete disorder and will not come as a result of magical practices, nor of a natural shock, nor of a friendly understanding. Decolonizing educational leadership is not being offered as a panacea or yet another diversity or equity, diversity and inclusion (EDI) project, but as an alternative way of leading schools that will intentionally see schools as part of the resistance to modern forms of colonization, disrupting white supremacy, settler colonialism, and taking back what was lost, not only in Western countries, but emerging contexts such as Jamaica, Kenya, Brazil, India, and all the spaces that Europeans colonized and stole not only, land but cultures and knowledge. Decolonizing theorizing, practice, pedagogies, and ways of knowing is about reclaiming of geographies and spaces of knowledge and knowing (Abdi, 2012).

Embracing new philosophies of education is not easy. Educators must be intentional about wanting to change. Education in Western countries and the Global South have not always identified the legacies of colonialism thereby creating inequities in education. Eurocentric knowledge has been posited as objective, reproduced in texts, dominate leadership theorizing and practice, perpetuated and is kept in place by predominantly white professors in academia. "Coloniality, is still the most general form of domination in the world today" (Abdi, 2012, p. 170), perpetuates the hegemony of the dominant with chilling consequences for those in schools.

coloniality of power is based upon 'racial' social classification of the world population under Eurocentered world power. But coloniality of power is not exhausted in the problem of 'racist' social relations. It pervaded and modulated the basic instances of the Eurocentered capitalist colonial/modern world power to become the cornerstone of this coloniality of power (Quijano, 2007, p. 171).

Coloniality gains power through classifications of people based on aspects of identity and manifested through white supremacy. White supremacy is a mechanism of social control that was developed through Eurocentered world power (Martinot, 2010; Painter, 2010). The construct of race and white supremacy in the creation of social hierarchies reinforced the alliance between white people in lower socioeconomic class with those in the ruling class (Battalora, 2015). Today, the power of coloniality has not been exhausted and exists in schooling practices as well as the wider society. White supremacy is the cornerstone of coloniality.

The goal of decolonizing education is to decenter Eurocentric ideology and cultural systems and recenter of knowledge of Indigenous and other colonized peoples that have been displaced. Destabilizing coloniality in education is an unsettling and uncomfortable necessity. That does not mean this work must be done without empathy or care, but refraining from confronting coloniality in direct, assertive ways continues to enact hubris; it privileges the comfort of the white colonial mind over the affective well-being and historical suffering of the subaltern (Domínguez, 2019). Educational leaders must work to achieve ontological distance from life in postcolonial systems, but this work need not be mired in guilt or drudgery (Domínguez, 2019). Coloniality resides in the day-to-day realities of education and schooling. It appears through neoliberal polices of meritocracy, acts of racial discrimination, misogyny, patriarchy, homophobia, and transphobia and other forms of oppression (Dutro & Bien, 2014). How schools are organized and the philosophy that guides education must change to dismantle the hold of coloniality and the ways it is manifested. It is the hope that educational leaders will create imageries for themselves that do not rest on coloniality and white supremacy, and new epistemologies will be drawn on to confront, disrupt, and mediate the ways in which coloniality resides in schools, and impacts the lives of BIPOC students and staff. The aim is to engage educational leaders in more liberatory ways of being, engage with complex and critical ontological assumptions, and explore alternative leadership theorizing and praxis.

Like Domínguez (2019), I argue that intentionality matters to disrupt normative assumptions about education, yet enacting decolonizing educational leadership and embracing new epistemologies should not be an act of drudgery, but of joy, hope, and possibility. Ultimately, such imaginative work might expose the many ways that coloniality works through educational leaders and schools while generating practical, decolonial ways educators can engage in teaching, leading, and learning. By understanding coloniality, educational leaders are better able to see why it is necessary and important to disrupt the reliance on Eurocentric ways of knowing in schools. While acknowledging the diversity of critical theoretical narratives and approaches to decolonizing education, there is also a need for continued critical, intellectual, and practical discourses about coloniality. Current educational and schooling practices cannot be understood without understanding coloniality. This is a precursor to engaging in decolonization.

Conclusion

Coloniality happens in previously colonized spaces and in spaces not historically colonized but subdued by allure of Eurocentrism. Coloniality continues to shape global structure of economic and cultural relations of power (Oyedemi, 2020). Oyedemi argues as well that racialization of the body and ubiquitous in current discourses is a core constituent of coloniality, and that race stands in the center of colonial structure of the idea of cultural superiority and economic domination in the system of capitalism. Through coloniality anti-Black racism is perpetuated. "The social construction of race forms a key element in social classification of the colonized and the colonizers, with a resultant effect on a relationship of power that created superior and inferior groups, supported with pseudoscientific 'evidence' to invent race and justify racial hierarchy" (Oyedemi, 2020, p. 401). If educational leaders are to meet the challenges of the twenty-first-century education and schooling, addressing inequities, system racism, and other forms of oppression, and coloniality must be named and addressed.

REFERENCES

Abdi, A. A. (2012). Oral societies and colonial experiences: Sub-Saharan Africa, and the de-facto power of the written word. *International Education, 37*(1), 42–59.

Battalora, J. (2015). *Birth of a White nation: The invention of White people and its relevance today.* Singapore: Strategic Book Publishing and Rights Co. LLC..

De L'Estolle, B. (2008). The past as it lives now: An anthropology of colonial legacies. *Social Anthropology, 16*(3), 267–279.

Domínguez, M. (2019). Decolonial innovation in teacher development: Praxis beyond the colonial zero-point. *Journal of Education for Teaching, 45*(1), 47–62.

Dutro, E., & Bien, A. C. (2014). Listening to the speaking wound: A trauma studies perspective on student positioning in schools. *American Educational Research Journal, 51*(1). https://doi.org/10.3102/0002831213503181.

Fanon, F. (1963). *The wretched earth.* New York: Grove Press.

Garcia, G. A., & Natividad, N. D. (2018). Decolonizing leadership practices: Towards equity and justice at Hispanic-Serving institutuons (HSIs) and emerging (eHSIs). *Journal of Transformative Leadership and Policy Studies, 7*(2), 25–39.

Majumdar, N. (2017). Silencing the subaltern: Resistance & gender in postcolonial theory. *Catalyst, 1*(1). Retrieved from https://catalyst-journal.com/vol1/no1/silencing-the-subaltern

Maldonado-Torres, N. (2007). On the coloniality of being: Contributions to the development of a concept. *Cultural Studies, 21*(2–3), 240–270.

Maldonado-Torres, N. (2011). Thinking through the decolonial turn: Post-continental interventions in theory, philosophy, and critique—An introduction. *Transmodernity: Journal of Peripheral Cultural Production of the Luso-Hispanic World, 1*(2) Retrieved from https://escholarship.org/uc/item/59w8j02x.

Martinot, S. (2010). *The machinery of whiteness: Studies in the structure of racialization.* Philadelphia, PA: Temple University Press.

Mendoza, B. (2015). Coloniality of gender and power: From post-coloniality to decoloniality. In L. Disch & M. Hawkesworth (Eds.), *The Oxford handbook of feminist theory.* New York: Oxford University Press.

Mignolo, W. (2009). Dispensable and bare lives: Coloniality and the hidden political/economic agenda of modernity: Human architecture. *Journal of the Sociology of Self-Knowledge, 7*(2), Article 7. Retrieved from https://scholarworks.umb.edu/humanarchitecture/vol7/iss2/7

Okihiro, G. (2014). *Margins and mainstreams: Asians in American history and culture.* Seattle, WA: University of Washington Press.

Oyedemi, T. (2020). (De)coloniality and South African academe. *Critical Studies in Education, 61*(4), 399–415.

Painter, J. (2010). Rethinking territory. Antipode. *A Radical Journal of Geography,* *42*(5), 1090–1118. https://doi.org/10.1111/j.1467-8330.2010.00795.x.

Patel, L. (2014). *Countering coloniality in educational research: From ownership to answerability.* London: Zed Books.

Quijano, A. (2000). Coloniality of power and eurocentrism in Latin America. *International Journal of Progressive Human Services, 30*(2), 148–164.

Quijano, A. (2007). Coloniality and modernity/rationality. *Cultural Studies, 21*(2–3), 168–178.

Simmons, M., & Dei, G. J. S. (2012). Reframing anti-colonial theory for the diasporic context. *Postcolonial Directions in Education, 1*(1), 67–99.

Tuck, E., & Yang, K. W. (2012). Decolonization is not a metaphor. *Decolonization: Indigeneity, Education & Society, 1*(1), 1–40.

Tucker, K. (2018). Unraveling coloniality in international relations: Knowledge, relationality, and strategies for engagement. *International Political Sociology, 12,* 215–232.

Velez, V., & Tuana, N. (2020). Editors' introduction Tango dancing with María Lugones: Toward decolonial feminisms. *Critical Philosophy of Race, 8*(1–2), 1–24.

CHAPTER 4

Decolonizing the Mind: Process of Unlearning, Relearning, Rereading, and Reframing for Educational Leaders

Abstract This chapter examines what it means to decolonize the mind. I draw on the work of Ngũgĩ wa Thiong'o, Kenyan writer and academic, who wrote *Decolonizing the Mind: The Politics of Language*. The chapter also examines how school leaders might use unlearned ways of knowing and practices that are harmful to students, and how this examination leads to relearning, rereading, and reframing of knowledge and practice. Different ways of decolonizing the mind are explored which includes naming, reflection, and action. The chapter ends with a call for action.

Keywords Decolonizing the mind • Decolonizing process • Unlearning • Relearning • Rereading • Reframing • Transformative action

Introduction

Drawing on the work of Ngũgĩ wa Thiong'o and his seminal book *Decolonising the Mind: The Politics of Language in African Literature*, I suggest in this volume that it is important for educational and school leaders to decolonize their minds as a precursor to engaging in decolonizing educational leadership practices. I argue that decolonizing educational leadership is important to creating change in the lives of all students and in particular Black, Indigenous, People of Color (BIPOC) students, by influencing policy and enacting critical leadership approaches. wa Thiong'o (2020) in a recent speech talked about the importance of Indigenous languages in his own upbringing. "Mother Wanjik?, wherever your soul rests, I beg you to forgive me for all the years I had abandoned the tongue you gave me at birth; the language through which you sang me lullabies; and told me stories that thrilled the heart. I have come back home: I embrace my mother tongue. The prodigal son is back." To decolonize the mind educators must unlearn, reread, and relearn history beyond the purview of the colonizers (Daniels, 2018). It is important that educational leaders understand the complexities of a decolonizing approach within contemporary spaces of learning, teaching, and human well-being (Abdi, 2007), and decolonize their minds before embarking on the journey of decolonizing their leadership practice.

Too often we witness school leaders who say they are doing culturally responsive, culturally appropriate, social justice education but who still hold notions of meritocracy, unwilling to challenge the system and scratch at the surface of inequity. They stretch themselves to accommodate neoliberal educational policies such as standardization and efforts to privatize public education. One of the tools of control for the colonizers was the breaking of the mind and spirit, making the colonized lose confidence in themselves and their ancestral knowledge. Examples of colonized minds are present today in people who live in former colonies. In Jamaica, for example, lighter skinned people are called 'browning', elevated and seen as having more social capital, the local dialect patois is frowned upon in some areas as a means of communicating in favor of English. Those who speak the 'Queen's' English are seen as more knowledgeable and educated. Wane (2019) in asking the question *Is Decolonizing the Spirit Possible?* suggests that "in the case of Africans, education became a weapon with which to cultivate the intellectual of the Africans" (p. 17). Through this control the colonized live their lives mimicking the colonizer, desiring to be like their master (Memmi, 2013).

Education was used as a tool for control through the knowledge that was taught in schools in the colonies. In places like Jamaica, while I attended high school, I was taught about wheat on the Prairies, but nothing about Timbuktu in Mali—home of one of the great trading posts and center of commerce in Africa. In educational materials, the continent of Africa and Africans were represented in mainly negative ways so that the colonized would distance themselves from the knowledge of their ancestor. In many instances that colonization of the mind was successful as some Black people continue to deny their African heritage.

Unlearning, Relearning, Rereading, and Reframing

Practice can be transformed through the process of learning, unlearning, rereading, and reframing. While these notions achieve similar goals of allowing scholars and practitioners to draw on new knowledge, there are subtleties at each stage which will be explored in the chapter. Unlearning, relearning, rereading, and reframing are viewed as a circular process of knowledge creation that informs practice. Colonialism is embedded in the structures of education and dominance of hegemonic discourses. For new approaches to become embedded and sustained, and have the desired impact, some knowledge and ways of thinking and socialization will have to be unlearned, new concepts and theorizing learned, situations and understandings be reread, and practices change. Klein (2008) suggests unlearning involves letting go of deeply held assumptions and relearning is the process of creating new understandings and behaviors. This change in practice and understanding I conceptualize as reframing. Conditions and space must be created to support school leaders to engage in this kind of deep learning that create shift in practice and consciousness. I argue here that these are the necessary conditions for school leaders to work through unsettling hegemonic knowledge and practices that they have embraced. Ladson-Billings (1999) in her work with teachers developing culturally relevant teaching practices warned against 'episodic workshops' which are prevalent in education. Ladson-Billings (1999) suggests that in most schools opportunities for teacher learning and development have been limited to episodic workshops that, at best, introduce teachers to a new idea and gave them some supportive materials. In Ontario, Canada, educators and school leaders have been given workshops on culturally responsive pedagogy, antiracist education, equity and diversity training, and most recently anti-Black racism training. Despite the resources and time being spent on these workshops, it has not resulted in the desired changes in (a) reduction in the drop out and suspension rates of Black and Indigenous youths, and (b) change in attitudes of some administrators and teachers. Research show that systemic racism is widespread in some school boards in Ontario, Black and Indigenous students are dropping out and getting suspended at alarming rates, and there is a growing evidence of anti-Black racism at all levels education and schooling.

For school leaders attempting to implement a decolonizing vision of educational leadership, it is important to develop new kinds of knowledge and strategies to implement grounded in theory—praxis. I argue that this is a crucial determinant of success of their efforts. Ball and Cohen (1999) describe this type of content knowledge as including the "ways that ideas connect across fields and to everyday life" (p. 8). Decolonizing education is about changing schooling experiences of students who continue to be marginalized in the education system based on regimes of power and knowledge rooted in colonial and hegemonic mindset and knowledge. This requires building capacity of school leaders through processes of learning, unlearning, and relearning. Capacity building to support school leaders to implement decolonizing approaches to educational leadership is discussed more fully in Chap. 5.

The process of unlearning, relearning, rereading, and reframing is not without tensions. Questions often arise about space (where and how), and who is engaged with school leaders in this process. Some school boards in Ontario hire 'experts' to work with school leaders. This removes the vulnerability and tensions that can arise when practitioners who work in the same space or school have the responsibility of leading capacity and professional development. Drawing on the expertise of outsiders is a means of bringing new knowledge to school leaders (Klein, 1999). There might also be tensions with perceived power differentials based on who is asked to lead the process. There might also be tensions with outsiders participating in such deep dialogic processes that arise due to lack of understanding of the culture of the organization, notwithstanding that outside 'experts' might provide depth of knowledge that school leaders may lack. This insider and outsider dynamic can impact the process, however valuing outsider knowledge over the contextualized understanding of school leaders can be problematic, sending a signal that their knowledge is somehow secondary (Klein, 1999). The difficult question has always been how to draw on and include the knowledge that school leaders have built up through their experiences, while disrupting racist, stereotypical, and Eurocentric views that they may hold. It is important to build on the *a priori* knowledge of school leaders. These are the complexities of shifting mindset and philosophy, with the intent of changing the practices of those involved in critical education of decolonizing, theorizing, and practice.

Reframing refers to the process of changing the focus of a situation or problem and examining it from different perspectives. Research with school leaders in Jamaica, Kenya and the Greater Toronto Area (GTA) reveal that, school leaders who engaged in deep reflective process of unlearning and relearning were able to change or infleuce their practice positive ways. As they became more agentive so did some of the teachers that they worked with in their efforts to address inequities in the schooling experience of students (see Lopez, 2015, 2016). Arriaza and Kroevtz (2006) in their research with teachers on ways to reframe teaching and learning to achieve more equity in schools suggest:

> What is needed is a new kind of leadership, principals who are willing to commit to leading for student accomplishment, for organizational health, for professional learning, and for long-range and deep improvements. These leaders work seriously to support the transformation of schooling and teaching and understand the importance of helping to build a learning community that includes all teachers and students. These are not "lone rangers" who depend on charisma and individual genius to transform schools. Rather, they are collaborative learners and teachers [school leaders] who advocate for democratic principles. (p. 2)

Organizations that will truly excel in the future will be the organizations that discover how to tap people's commitment and capacity to learn at all levels in an organization (Senge, 2000).

Process of Decolonizing

The process of decolonizing begins with self and educators must begin with themselves. Absolon (2019) suggests that, "decolonizing education is for educators who want to develop their capacity to understand their own location vis-à-vis colonization and journey toward unpacking and unlearning their internalization of colonial ideologies ...it enables one to take inventory of one's path and further determine what shifts are necessary" (p. 14). This requires a shift in mind and spirit. It is not just doing the work, it also thinking about the work and the impact on students as well as self. As Smith (2016) suggests at the centre. At the center of change is the mind and spirit. In order for decolonization to happen educational leaders and educators must develop critical consciousness and adopt an agentic mindset when engaging with Indigenous students and all students who are marginalized by the education system (Berryman et al., 2015). This process requires flexibility in thinking and challenges educational leaders to accept multiple ways of knowing by drawing on various perspectives. This critical knowledge can also become a source of hope and action that pushes people to challenge inequities in all aspects of schooling. Developing critical consciousness involves change in knowledge and perspectives which involves reflection, political efficacy, and critical action (Christens, Winn, & Duke, 2016). Decolonization internally means a disruption of the very belief system one has come to know (Absolon, 2019). Kanu (2006) argues that it is imperative that educators decolonize the space of education, but in order for us to do so we must decolonize the mind.

Decolonization is a systemic rejection of colonialism through a critical encounter and examination of the dominance and hegemonic knowledge, representation, and theory used in teaching and learning within education. Decolonization cannot happen when educators or educational leaders think about Indigenous [and other students] from a deficit perspective (Smith, 2016). Students must be seen through the lens of what they can do, and the strengths that they bring and can build from. Smith suggests further that building capacity of Indigenous educators and educational leaders is of utmost importance in the quest for decolonization of education. In the endeavor of decolonizing the mind there is much for educators to learn from their own histories as and Indigenous scholars. It is the hope that this book will support educational leaders to build capacity and become agentive in decolonizing education and educational leadership in particular. As mentioned before in this volume, the starting point of decolonization is understanding coloniality, and how it is manifested in self, education, and schooling. I draw on the work of Absolon (2019) to highlight some of the actions that educational and school leaders can engage in as they embark on a journey to decolonize their minds. These are doing doable actions that can be done personally or with a group of critical friends on a similar journey. Absolon (2019)—an Anishinaabek scholar—describes the decolonization process as involving nine steps. She argues to decolonize is to (p. 17):

- *Detoxify* and cleanse from the internalization of a colonized mindset about what informs what we teach, how we teach, and how we teach methods and theories of practice;
- *Question*, to wonder, to rethink and retheorize how, what, and why we practice, teach, and research the way we do;
- *Cleanse* one's spirit, heart, mind, and body from the toxins of colonial knowledge, teaching, and learning;

- *Question* the norms and status quo of the application of theories and methods within Anisinaabek peoples [and other peoples] community;
- *Become uncomfortable* in the detoxing;
- *Engage* in a journey of learning from Anishinaabek perspectives what colonization looks like and how it is seeded into every fabric of life;
- *Return to the land*;
- *Restore* respect to Mother Earth, water, and all forms of human life; and
- *Reject* being a host of colonization.

While these nine actions are listed I see them as operating in a fluid, interative, generative and circular manner that all educators engage with over time. Indigenous and non-Indigenous people can use this decolonization process as a guide to support their journey. The process starts with self, uprooting and removing the colonial thoughts and mindset.

Disruption of Colonial Mentality

Decolonization of the mind is essential to engaging in decolonizing education. One cannot enter decolonizing practice holding beliefs that uphold white supremacy, patriarchy, and neoliberal notions of education and schooling. wa Thiong'o (1986) asserts in *Decolonizing the Mind* that the journey of decolonizing begins with self. Many in the field of education and elsewhere draw on his seminal work *Decolonizing the Mind*, in which he elucidates' the subversion of African literature, language, and ways in which the ideas and language of the colonizer and imposed by the colonizer had a devastating impact on the minds of subalterns and people of Kenya. Strobel (1997) suggests that decolonization of the mind is a process of reconnecting with the past to understand the present and involves dislodging of colonial mentality that some hold. Educators must work to examine the impact of what David and Okazaki (2006) refer to as the 'colonial mentality' in their work. Colonial mentality is manifested through feelings of ethnic and cultural inferiority that places the values, attitudes, beliefs, and behaviors of the dominant/colonizing culture over one's own culture.

Nandy (1997) in his writings examined the idea of a second colonization in India after its independence and suggested that some who fought against colonialism seemingly embraced what he refers to as the 'second colonialism' where "modern Indians have stabilized their modern self by internalizing the colonial ideology of the state they confronted in the nineteenth century" (p. 227). Growing up in Jamaica—a former British colony—the colonial mentality was and is exhibited in all aspects of life including education, where British customs and traditions were and still are in some spaces elevated over Jamaican customs grounded in our African ancestry. Colonial mentality is a form of internalized racial oppression, where a person internally incorporates the idea that they are less than another person or entity (David & Okazaki, 2006). Internalized oppression can have "negative psychological and mental health consequences" (David, 2013, p. 62).

Through internalized colonialism oppressed people instead of rising up against the oppressors and colonizers acquiesce to the "cultural imposition of the dominant group on the minority groups, and cultural disintegration of the oppressed group's indigenous culture" (David, 2013, p. 57). The dominant group is given power to define and name reality, determine what is 'normal,' 'real,' and 'correct,' and ignore, discount, misrepresent, or eradicate the culture, language, and history of those that they position as the 'other' (Speight, 2007). In education in Canada and Western countries this is manifested through complicity, the elevation of knowledge of the dominant culture in curriculum, teaching, leading, learning, classroom practices, and policies. For example, the continued reliance on canonical texts written by, what some describe, 'dead White men' and resistance to include in curricula texts written by Black, Brown, and Indigenous people. The histories and experiences of colonized groups continue to be marginalized in education and schooling and the discourse of the dominant posited as the preferred epistemology and ways of knowing.

Strobel (1997) suggests that decolonization of the mind takes place in three phases. The first phase is '*naming.*' "To decolonize is to be able to name internalized oppression, shame, inferiority, confusion, and anger" (p. 66). In my own work in challenging forms of oppression I suggest that educators must name the issue in order to engage in actions of disruption and dislodging that will result in lasting and sustainable change. Educators and school leaders cannot fix what they cannot name. The second phase is '*reflection.*' "To decolonize is to develop the ability to question one's reality as constructed by colonial narratives" (p. 66). This involves questioning one's complicity in creating space for colonial and hegemonic discourses and/or leaving those narratives and discourses in spaces unchallenged it is important to 'call out' and sometimes 'call in'. In the reflective stance it might be necessary to support others to engage in self reflexivity by 'calling out' actions that are detrimental to students and the well-being of others, and inviting others into dialogic conversation to advance learning 'calling in'.

It is important that people see BIPOC in positions of leadership. Intentional changes must be made in organizations to make this happen. BIPOC educators must be supported in developing the necessary skills and knowledge to assume these leadership positions. Oftentimes aggressions within organizations (micro-aggressions) thwart the professional development of Black, Indigenous, and People of Color who have been positioned on the margins. Empowerment means challenging systems to create space and new voices and knowledge. This is a process that builds overtime starting with 'Naming' and ending with 'Action' (see Fig. 4.1).

The process of decolonization requires praxis, that is, connecting theory to action. Aristotle (2003) saw praxis as a form of conscious, self-aware action. Kemmis (2010) suggests that the term 'praxis' can be used in the Aristotelian sense or in the post-Marxian sense. "Educational action is a species of praxis in both these senses because, on the one side, it involves the morally informed and committed action of those who practise education, and, on the other, it helps to shape social formations and conditions as well as people and their ideas, their commitments and their consciousness" (p. 10). I have had to embark on a journey of decolonizing my own mind, shedding the colonial knowledge that formed my schooling experiences growing up in Jamaica. It is an ongoing process of learning, unlearning, relearning, and reframing informed by new knowledge and experiences. As a Black woman, born and raised in Jamaica, descendant of the enslaved, my own ancestral knowledge was denied me, and what I came to understand as legitimate knowledge was a Westernized, White Supremacist, Christian, colonial, and patriarchal world system (hooks, 2000). As educators embark on this journey they must find spaces to heal the colonial wounds that are not only in the past, but present in everyday experiences.

Fanon (1963) noted that "independence has certainly brought the colonized people's moral reparation and recognized their dignity. But they have not yet had time to elaborate a society or build and ascertain values"

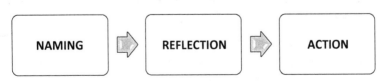

Fig. 4.1   Phases of decolonization (Adapted from Strobel, 1997)

(p. 40). Fanon argued further that the violence inflicted upon the colonized left deep psychological wounds on the mind and being that manifested in a variety of ways including what some call 'mental colonization' or 'colonial mentality' which is the perception of cultural inferiority and some would argue a form of racialized oppression (Bulhan, 1985) as mentioned elsewhere in this volume in addition. In order to resist, find liberation and hope, the task of liberation from colonial oppression must include decolonization of the land, but also decolonization of the mind (Fanon, 1963). Adams, Kurtis, Gomez, Molina, and Dobles (2018) in examining the impact of Fanon's work and contributions to decolonizing the mind discourse suggest, that for Fanon "the task of mental decolonization was not primarily an abstract, theoretical concern; instead, it was a necessary component in the process of political and existential liberation whereby the 'wretched of the earth' take direction of their lives, bodies, spirits" (Fanon, 1963, p. 37).

As I reflect on my own work as an educator, I see hope, promise, and transformative actions in a decolonizing approach and framework not only for myself but for other educators as well. Decolonization is about developing and sharpening our thinking processes and pursuing transformative change, breaking with dominant practices and resisting subordination in all forms, and about the ability to define one's own agenda for a new future (Dei & Jaimungal, 2018). All journey focused on dismantling systems of oppression and decolonization begins with self, and taking time to reflect and grow in one's identity before engaging in the work is important (Absolon, 2012). The cultivating of an ethnic sense of self creates space to resist dominant structures, and the stabilization of an ethnic identity is a healing and transformative act in response of a people who have been "deeply violated" (Strobel, 2005, p. 28).

When we examine our lived experiences as school leaders we are forced to confront colonization and its impact not only on our lives but the lives of students we serve. Through the examination of our experiences we are able to explore ways of healing and new forms of knowledge. It is a process where we come to understand what we need to learn and unlearn. It is also a space where some educators begin to acknowledge their privileged positions, and as settlers, and their complicity in colonial practices. Through self-reflexivity educators begin the journey of understanding how colonialism continues to operate in daily life and deepen their understanding of how their own complicity with these and other colonial discourses and regimes of truth (McGregor, 2014) impact others as we seek to work in ethically informed, relational ways. Self-reflexivity helps to dislodge ways of Western epistemic norms that have devalued other ways of knowing and open spaces for learning and relearning.

wa Thiong'o (1986) argues that colonialism makes the colonized see their past as wasteland of nonachievement and makes them want to distance themselves from it. However we can reconnect through the decolinizing process. Asher (2005) argues that decolonization is a self-reflexive process requiring the deconstruction of not only the colonizer and external oppressive structures, but also one's own internalization of and participation in same. As school leaders engage in the decolonizing process they are encouraged to keep a journal to log their journey and stories of how they came to take up decolonizing discourse and the challenges along the way. Decolonizing work is never done alone but in collaboration with others. Sharing this journey can help others to rethink and reimagine critical education theorizing and practices. Educators who are engaging in social justice, antiracist, culturally responsive education, and other critical discourses do not have to discard the knowledge gained from those discourses but use it to inform decolonizing practices. Shultz (2012) in *Decolonizing Social Justice Education: From Policy Knowledge to Citizenship Action* noted that overtime she began to worry about the meaning of social justice as declarations emerged from such disparate places as conservative governments education documents, activist networks, international organizations, and even from the offices of a few corporations that name social justice in their efforts to project images of sustainability. The same concerns are arising in context of social unrest in 2020 and people are rising up to demand justice and the organizations are making statements in support of greater equity and challenging anti-Black racism, but nothing materially changes in how these organizations operate. Shultz (2012) argues not for abandonment of social justice as framework for action but reclamation of the term to signify activism and social transformation.

Through the process of decolonizing the mind colonized peoples engage in an ontological process of reclaiming their identity, self-worth, histories, language, rituals, art, philosophies, and social power (Schwimmer, 2004). Schwimmer asserts that it is mostly through education and schooling grounded on Eurocentric and Western ways of knowing that much of the colonization of mind has taken place, impacting knowledge, conceptions, values, and language as well as social institutions. A focus of educational leadership is influencing policy creation at government levels and implementing policies at the school level. These conversations must include decolonizing approaches. The glaring omission of coloniality from educational administration and leadership discourse over the years necessitates a review, acknowledgment of this omission, and redress. Achieving a decolonizing perspective involves reflexivity that supports educational leaders to understand coloniality, how it is reproduced in education, as well as expanding notions of education and leadership to include voices and experiences that have not traditionally been reflected in educational administration (Samier, 2005). This includes going beyond the content of education and the activities taking place within educational establishments; it involves the whole process of the acquisition and transmission of knowledge, the philosophies underlying education, values, and worldview they inculcate (Samier, 2005).

Bhabha (1994) argues that the narratives of history must be changed, our sense of what it means to live, and the interruption of Western discourses that have displaced subaltern narratives and the critical theoretical perspectives they bring to educational administration and leadership discourse. The problem with representing authentically other cultures that have been under colonization is transcending the colonized self that is created in the process (Samier, 2005). The process of decolonizing the mind includes what Samier (2005) describes as destroying the 'cultural bomb' that colonizers and Eurocentric knowledge uses to effectively destroy 'cultural bomb,' that effectively destroy people's belief in themselves, their names, languages, their environment, heritage of their struggle, their unity, and their capacities to embrace who they truly want and ought to be given their contexts of living on this earth. The 'cultural bomb' makes people see their past as one wasteland of nonachievement and it makes them want to distance themselves from that wasteland and makes them want to identify with that which is furthest removed from themselves, for instance, with other peoples' languages rather than their own (Quijano, 2007). This involves reclaiming of self and identities. School leaders have a role to play in not only reclaiming their identities, but supporting BIPOC students to reclaim their identities as well. This means a change in how educational policies are constructed and implemented, and in curriculum and pedagogy and all aspects of schooling.

CONCLUSION

In conclusion, it is important to disrupt and unpack colonial vestiges in educational leadership and policy, and educators must decolonize their minds. Decolonizing the mind is an attempt to free those who occupy spaces that were once colonized of the thinking and practices that once kept their voices and experiences out of the center of educative enterprises, such as schools. It is the hope that school leaders, and indeed all educators, engage on a journey of unlearning, relearning, rereading, and reframing notions of school leadership grounded in more liberatory approaches, and engage in thinking and practices that reject dominance of Eurocentric and hegemonic knowledge. As wa Thiong'o argued, the success of the colonizer was having the colonized "sing their praises," while they emptied Africa of its resources. This is the mindset that must be dislodged. wa Thiongo's provocation in decolonizing the mind calls on educators to assess their professional commitments.

I conclude this chapter by drawing on the words of Marie Battiste (2013), who expressed a hope for all educators, not just Indigenous educators:

> For educators, Aboriginal[1] or not, it is not enough to rebel against injustices unless we also rebel against our lack of imagination and caring. To understand education, one must love it or care deeply about learning, and accept it as a legitimate process for growth and change. To accept education as it is however, is to betray it. To accept education without betraying it, you must love it for those values that show what it might become. You have to have enough love of learning to have the courage to remake it, imagine it, and teach it....Decolonizing education, then, is the act of love that generates ...passion and activism ...it is, then a call for action for all educators to take on as well. (pp. 190–191)

Decolonization is an unfolding and ongoing process that takes place on multiple levels, personally, structurally, and systematically. I believe that conditions in schools that marginalize and exclude some students will not change unless theory is connected to practice. In Chap. 5, I explore some

---

[1] Aboriginal refers to the first inhabitants of Canada, and includes First Nations, Inuit, and Métis peoples. This term came into popular usage in Canadian contexts after 1982, when Section 35 of the Canadian Constitution defined the term as such. In recent years the term has been contested and Indigenous is more often used to describe the First Peoples of Canada.

specific ways that decolonizing leadership practices can be implemented by school leaders at all levels in schools. It does not mean that principals, vice principals, and teacher leaders stop their ongoing critical work, but that they seek to find convergences. Educational leaders must be intentional in naming the ongoing structures of colonialism that are present in schools and education systems in Western nations and the Global South. This is an urgent call to school leaders to reflect on practice and change course, as current discourses of equity and diversity have not yielded the required results.

REFERENCES

Abdi, A. A. (2007). Oral societies and colonial experiences: Sub-Saharan Africa, and the de-facto power of the written word. *International Education, 37*(1), 42–59.

Absolon, K. (2012). *Kaandossiwin: How we come to know.* Halifax, Nova Scotia: Fernwood Publishing.

Absolon, K. (2019). Indigenous wholistic theory: A knowledge set for practice. *First Peoples Child and Family Review, 14*(1) 22–42.

Adams, G., Kurtis, T., Gomez, L., Molina, L. E., & Dobles, I. (2018). Decolonizing knowledge in hegemonic psychological science. In N. Wane & K. Todd (Eds.), *Decolonial pedagogy: Examining sites of resistance, resurgence, and renewal* (pp. 35–56). Cham, Switzerland: Palgrave Macmillan.

Aristotle. (2003). Ethics. Trans. [1953] J. A. K. Thompson, revised with notes and appendices [1976] *Hugh Tredennick, with an introduction, Jonathon Barnes, and preface,* A. C. Grayling. London: The Folio Society.

Arriaza, G., & Kroevtz, M. L. (2006). *Collaborative teacher leadership: How teachers can foster equitable schools.* Thousand Oaks, CA: Corwin Press.

Asher, N. (2005). At the interstices: Engaging post colonial and feminist perspectives for a multicultural educatiion pedagoy in the South. *Teachers College Record, 107,* 1079–1106.

Ball, D. L., & Cohen, D. K. (1999). Developing practice, developing practitioners: Toward a practice-based theory of professional education. In L. Darling-Hammond & G. Sykes (Eds.), *Teaching as the learning profession: Handbook of policy and practice* (pp. 3–31). San Francisco: Jossey-Bass.

Battiste, M. (2013). *Decolonizing education: Nourishing the learning spirit.* Saskatoo, SK: Purich Publishing.

Berryman, M., Carr-Stewart, S. B., Kovach, M., & Steeves, L. E. (2015). *Seeking their vocies: Improving Indogenous student learning outcomes.* Regina, SK: Saskatchewan. Instructional DEvelopment and Researh Unit.

Bhabha, Homi K. (1994). *The Location of Culture*. New York and London: Routledge.

Bulhan, H. A. (1985). *Frantz Fanon and the psychology of oppression*. New York: Plenum.

Christens, B. D., Winn, L. T., & Duke, A. M. (2016). Empowerment and critical consciousness: A conceptual cross-fertilization. *Adolescent Research Review, 1*, 15–27.

Daniel, B.-J. (2018). Knowing thr self and the reson for being: Navigating racism in the academy. *Canadian Women Studies/Les cahiers de la femme, 32*(1–2), 59–66.

David, E. J. R. (2013). *Brown skin, white minds: Filipino-/American postcolonial psychology*. Information Age Publishing, Inc.

David, E. J. R., & Okazaki, S. (2006). The colonial mentality scale (CMS) for Filipino Americans: Scale construction and psychological implications. *Journal of Counseling Psychology, 53*(2), 241–252.

Dei, G. S. J., & Jaimungal, C. (2018). *Indigeneity and decolonial resistance: Alternatives to colonial thinking*. Graham, ME: Myers Education Press.

Fanon, F. (1963). *The wretched Earth*. New York: Grove Press.

hooks, b. (2000). *Feminist theory: From margin to center*. Boston, MA: South End Press.

Kanu, Y. (2006). *Curriculum as cultural practice: Postcolonial imaginations*. Toronto, ON: University of Toronto Press.

Kemmis, S. (2010). Research for praxis: knowing doing. *pedagogy. Culture & Society, 18*(1), 9–27.

Klein, E. J. (2008). Learning, unlearning, and relearning: Lessons from one school's approach to creating and sustaining learning communities. *Teacher Education Quarterly, Winter*, 80–97. Retrieved from https://www.montclair.edu/profilepages/media/1411/user/PDF_copy.pdf

Klein, S. R. (1999, January). Creating artful leadership. *International Journal of Leadership in Education, 2*(1), 23–30.

Ladson-Billings, G. (1999). Preparing teachers for diverse student populations: A critical-race theory perspective. *Review of Research in Education, 24*, 211–247.

Lopez, A. E. (2015). Navigating cultural borders in diverse contexts: building capacity through culturally responsive leadership and critical praxis. *Multicultural Education Review*, 1–14.

Lopez, A. E. (2016). *Culturally responsive and socially just leadership: From theory to action*. New York, NY: Palgrave Macmillan.

McGregor, C. (2014, Spring). Disrupting colonial mindsets: The power of learning networks. *In Education, 19*(3), 89–107.

Memmi, A. (2013). *The colonizer and the colonized*. London: Routledge.

Nandy, A. (1997). The decolonization of the mind. In M. Rahnema & V. Bowtree (Eds.), *The post-development reader*. London: Zed Books.

Quijano, A. (2007). Coloniality and modernity/rationality. *Cultural Studies, 21*(2–3) 168–178.

Samier, E. (2005). Toward public administration as a humanities discipline: A humanistic manifesto. *Halduskultuur, 6,* 6–59.

Schwimmer, E. (2004). Preface: In J. Clammer, S. Poirier, & E. Schwimmer (Eds.). The Nature of Nature. In *Figured Worlds: Ontological Obstacles in Intercultural Relations* (pp. ix–xii). Toronto: University of Toronto Press.

Senge, P. (2000). *Schools that learn: A fifth discipline field book for educators, parents, and everyone who cares about education.* New York: Doubleday.

Shultz, L. (2012). Decolonizing social justice education: From policy knowledge to citizenship action. In A. A. Abdi (Ed.), *Decolonizing philosophies of education* (pp. 29–42). Rotterdam, Netherlands: Sense Publishers.

Smith, T. (2016). Make space for indigeneity: Decolonizing education. *SELU Research Review Journal, 1*(2), 49–59.

Speight, S. L. (2007). Internalized racism: One more piece of the piece of the puzzle. *The Counseling Psychologist, 35,* 126–134.

Strobel, L. M. (1997). Coming full circle: Narratives of decolonization among post-1965 Filipino Americans. In M. P. P. Root (Ed.), *Filipino Americans: Transformation and identity.* Thousand Oaks, CA: Sage Publications.

Strobel, L. M. (2005). A personal story: Becoming a split Filipina subject. In De Jesus, M. L. (Ed.), *Pinay power: Peminist critical theory.* New York: Routledge.

wa Thiong'o, N. (1986). *Decolonising the mind: The politics of language in African literature.* London: J. Currey, Portsmouth; Heinemann.

wa Thiong'o, N. (2020). Address to global audience on September 5, 2020. Retrieved from https://www.standardmedia.co.ke/education/article/2001385255/walking-the-talk-ngugi-wa-thiong-o-addresses-a-global-audience-in-kikuyu

Wane, N. N. (2019). Is decolonizing the spirit possible? In N. N. Wane, M. S. Todorova, & K. Todd (Eds.), *Decolonizing the spirit in education and beyond: Resistance and solidarity.* Cham, Switzerland: Palgrave Macmillan.

CHAPTER 5

Restoring Capacity: Decolonizing Education and School Leadership Practices

Abstract This chapter discusses ways in which educational and school leaders can go about implementing decolonizing leadership. If change is to occur, then theory must be turned into action. It is an imperative to support school leaders to imagine what such a path might look like and support them on the journey. The chapter begins with a look at the capacity-building literature which is prevalent in school improvement discourse, but anchored in technocratic, neoliberal agenda and familiar to many school leaders. A turn is suggested towards the notion of restoring capacity to support decolonizing leadership, resting on the notion that communities and educators have knowledge. Notions of how this can be achieved are posited.

Keywords Capacity building • Self-reflexivity • Restoring capacity • Capacity promoting • Critical theorizing • Neoliberal education

INTRODUCTION

In this volume drawing on research that I conducted in Kenya (see Lopez & Rugano, 2018) and the Greater Toronto Area (see Lopez, 2015) with school leaders, my own journey as an educational and school leader, and the extant literature, I propose a framework that educational and school leaders might employ to support capacity development grounded in

© The Author(s), under exclusive license to Springer Nature Switzerland AG 2020
A. E. Lopez, *Decolonizing Educational Leadership*,
https://doi.org/10.1007/978-3-030-62380-7_5

decolonizing theorizing to support aspiring leaders, teacher leaders, and others. Those in educational leadership committed to decolonizing and other critical ideologies (anti-racist, culturally responsive, social justice), and to critical learning and leading must model ways in which this can happen (Garcia & Natividad, 2018).

Within a decolonized model of organizing and through a lens of decolonizing leadership practices, key questions to ask include "Who has the authority and decision-making power to promote and enact a decolonial education model grounded in equity, justice, and liberation for all?" (Garcia & Natividad, 2018, p. 31). Critical scholars, activists, and practitioners have also argued that the work and labor to change systems to be more responsive to the needs of marginalized people and challenge racism cannot rest on the shoulders of Black, Indigenous, and People of Color (BIPOC) alone. This has to be a shared responsibility of BIPOC educators and white educators, who in Ontario, Canada and many Western countries represent the majority of those in school leadership. If the goal of decolonizing educational leadership is for justice for all, and liberation, the oppressor and the oppressed must work together to disrupt coloniality of power that dictates how leaders manage and organize institutions (Freire, 1970).

Before expanding notions of capacity development that undergirds this chapter, I explore the capacity-building literature that is dominant in educational discourse. In the early 1990s scholars and educational leaders looked to different capacity-building models to enhance school improvement. Capacity development was built on these earlier notions of capacity building. The metaphor of 'making the turn' signals the shift I wish to make from capacity building to capacity development. Capacity development best suits decolonizing education as a process, and helps to inform leadership practices that might emerge.

CAPACITY BUILDING: MAKING THE TURN

The concept of capacity building came to prominence in the early 1990s in the context of national and international development (Dinham & Crowther, 2011). The notion of capacity building has been used to restructure schools to respond to the needs of a growing diverse student population. By building capacity school leaders embrace new approaches to leadership, and expand skills and knowledge. Efforts to improve school performance and through more effective leadership are not new. Many well-known scholars who research school effectiveness and school reform have posited various models to support schools effectiveness in responding to students. Over the years interest in school effectiveness and improvement has generated an abundance of literature that have explored a variety of theories, models, and methods for improving student learning, and signals a shift away from top-down mandates to more site-based and system-wide reform. Mitchell and Sackney (2000), Canadian scholars and theorists, suggest that building capacity at personal, interpersonal, and organizational levels is important in building capacity that will enhance the effectiveness of schools. To this end they suggest constructing professional knowledge and reducing dissonance between theory and practice. To achieve these goals, they suggest educators engage in critical reflection, establish professional network of critical friends, engage in team building and professional dialogue, and build trusting relationships.

Capacity building is multifaceted (Fullan, 2006), involving change in internal and external factors in schools (Stoll, 2009), and is dominant in the school improvement discourse. School improvement is seen as impossible without effective capacity building. Stoll (2009) argues that to achieve school improvement, the aim of which is to make a difference for students, the following are important for capacity building. Firstly, differentiated capacity-building approaches as schools' contexts vary and recognizes that schools are different. Capacity also varies within the wider contexts of school districts school boards. Stoll points to the nuanced approaches to capacity building. For example, in Ontario, Canada, school boards are offered supports to build capacity based on need, particular challenges achieving continuous improvement. Secondly, capacity building must include the broader aims of schooling and expand beyond supporting instructional improvement. Stoll argues that for a long time the focus was on what happens in classrooms and instructional strategies. However, focus should also be on student voice, the role of technology, and new understandings about what constitutes learning, issues such as student well-being, and capacity to live in an increasingly diverse world are emerging. As well, capacity development is seen as necessary to develop a more flexible workforce. Thirdly, capacity building should not be seen as static, but respond to current situations and issues that might arise in the future. Stoll (2009) suggests:

> Capacity building has to connect with a world order where...fast emerging technologies are affecting learning processes, and a new generation of

children and young people bring a different orientation that, in many cases, existing models of schooling may not meet. Judged by accountability systems, many school districts yearn to be free to offer curriculum and learning and teaching strategies they consider will provide the bedrock for future success. Teachers and school leaders, however, often find it difficult to devote attention to promoting creativity because of what they describe as "immense pressure" of focusing on standards or being 'very burdened by being driven by targets'. It requires a bold decision not to be constrained and to move away from 'rigidity' of some frameworks. Balancing being creative and innovative within the context of a standards approach, mixing "tried and tested' methods and experimentation isn't easy for most educators. (p. 10)

Today, in the era of educational, neoliberal policies, standardization, and efforts to curtail public education, school leaders in Western countries who work in public education in public education are faced with these challenges. Scripted curricula force teachers to teach to the test and school leaders are engulfed with an enormous agenda as they respond to the needs of students and communities. In this atmosphere it is difficult and challenging for school leaders to focus on capacity building as they are often responding to events of the day in their schools and the larger contextual environment. Reseearch conducted with school leaders in the GTA and Kenya reveal enormous workload which impacted their performance as school leaders. In the Global South school leaders are faced with a lack of resources, lack of training and sometimes necessary resources to be as effective as they would like to be. A lasting impact of colonialism particularly on the continent of Africa and the Global South is the continued lack of resources. Some countries on the continent of Africa are turning to China for much needed resouces and some worry that the emerging relationship is a form of neo-colonialism as these coutries become heavliy indebted to China.

Fourthly, to ensure sustainability of capacity-building efforts, Stoll (2009) argues there must be a 'habit of mind' to embrace change. Capacity for change is about learning with and from others. Stoll sees this kind of collaboration as essential to sustainability as well as supporting ongoing learning. Similar to critical pedagogies such as anti-racist education, anti-oppressive education, and culturally responsive education to address inequities in education and schooling, these initiatives are not sustainable if not embedded in practice and become part of everyday practice. Capacity building cannot be an 'add on'; it needs to be a 'habit of mind' (Hill, 1997). Fifthly, change in school systems and practices cannot be achieved by one person, and as such must be a collaborative effort, where developing leadership capacity must be across the entire system, what Fullan (2006) refers to as lateral capacity building. Lateral capacity building embraces the notion of collective responsibility and shared understanding of purpose, where people learn as a collective. While educators at the school might employ decolonizing leadership practices, more success will be gained, and chances of strategies becoming embedded and sustainable over time, requires that educational leaders at the system level also embrace a decolonizing leadership approach. Throughout my years as an educator and being involved in equity and critical education, when educators take on change by themselves, it is difficult to sustain and burn out sometimes occur. It is important that training training occur at all levels of the system.

Some argue that the notion of capacity building that emerged in 1990s emerged from neoliberal theorizing on organizational and community development. Eade and Williams (1995), as cited in Craig (2010), noted that 'capacity building' emerges from the international development literature as organizations responded to the need to democratize, and shift from 'top-down' approaches to development, in favor of strengthening people's capacity to determine their own values and priorities, and organize themselves to achieve this. "By the beginning of the twenty-first century, the notion of capacity building had become a powerful mobilizer of community development initiatives in both the majority and minority worlds. In many ways, the entry of this term—and the underlying philosophy and approach it was meant to capture—was a promising though problematic development" (Pence, 2015, p. 8). Pence (2015) argues further that capacity building and the related terminologies served to promote a technocratic neoliberal agenda and suggests:

> The underlying assumption of many international development initiatives, whether in ECD or other fields, is that the community, region, or country deemed in need of assistance 'lacks capacity' and that the donor or international development organization is in a position to provide that capacity, whether in the form of knowledge transfer, predefined outcomes, or managerial methods imported from the minority world. The question of whose capacity needs to be built, for what purpose, for whose benefit, and as identified by whom, is seldom raised, or is not explored in sufficient depth. Indeed, the use of the term capacity building is reminiscent of an earlier critique of the term 'underdevelopment.' (p. 8)

Pence notes furher that capacity-building initiatives focused on education and training are often based on a simple 'knowledge transfer' model, echoing Freire's (1972) critique of a 'banking' concept of education, that gives little or no space for mutual transformation in the learning process or for the contribution of local knowledges (Fanany et al. 2010).

The use of the metaphor 'making the turn' signals a shift away from neoliberal understandings of 'capacity development' to what Tedmanson (2003), an Australian Indigenous scholar, refers to 'restoring capacity.' I am shifting away from neoliberal notions of capacity building as these notions seek to lay the burden of change on individuals rather that systems and avoid challenging the Eurocentricity in education. As educators engage they must be mindful of the pitfalls neoliberal educational policies and approaches that are ubiquitous in education and some would argue embedded seamlessly in how education and schooling occurs. According to Tedmanson (2003) to restore capacity is to include in policy making the skills and knowledge of the community Connections with community, and acknowledging the role of community in education is an essential ingredient of decolonizing education:

> To restore capacity in our people is to [restore responsibility] for our own future. Notice that I talk of restoring rather than building capacity in our people ... we had 40 to 60,000 years of survival and capacity. The problem is that our capacity has been eroded and diminished [by white colonialists]—our people do have skills, knowledge and experience ... we are quite capable of looking after our own children and fighting for their future. (Tedmanson, 2003, p. 15)

The notion of 'restoring capacity' emerged from communities seeking to be in charge of their own learning. Restoring capacity within the context of educational and school leadership implies collaborative process that is respectful and inclusive grounded in decolonizing philosophies and practice. Other alternatives to capacity building includes what some call 'capacity building' to 'capacity promoting.' This approach was developed in partnership with First Nations communities in Canada and then utilized in co-development activities with numerous countries in sub-Saharan Africa (Pence, 2015).

RESTORING CAPACITY

Leaders must deconstruct colonial ways of knowing that are embedded within education and schooling. Educators in leadership roles, regardless of their skills and knowledge, cannot effect change by themselves and must collaborate with others. To ensure that changes are sustainable it is important to engage others a collaborative approach. This requires 'restoring capacity' that values the input of students and communities, education workers including teachers, teacher leaders, and administrators. With sociocultural and demographic shifts schools must restore capacity among staff where they act on their own agency to achieve the desired results. Calls to address systemic inequities and racism in education have required staff to engage in deep learning, acquire new knowledge, and for some dislodge knowledge that they have relied on for years, and which "have perpetuated colonizing mentalities into the 21st Century" (Pence, 2015, p. 10).

Restoring or promoting capacity is a crucial aspect of decolonizing education to ensure efforts do not become 'add ons' and are sustainable and embedded overtime. The path to engagin in and developing decolonizing education must be clear to those in educational leadership who want to embrace this approach and those who are aspiring to be leaders. The starting point of this process is educators examining their practice and reflecting on their philosophies and coming to an understanding of areas they need to learn and grow, and the kind of supports they need to achieve it. Restoring and promoting capacity geared toward improved outcomes for students is important if transformative change is to occur in schools. I suggest the following framework and areas as integral to 'restoring and promoting capacity' to support decolonizing educational leadership: (a) engage in self-reflexivity in relation to coloniality; (b) develop understanding of critical theorizing; (c) build relationships across communities; (d) engage in critical and difficult dialogue; (e) disrupt neoliberal educational polices; and (f) have action plan to sustain the journey. These ideas do not stand alone or happen in a linear fashion, but are in relationship with one another and are in motion and flow (see Fig. 5.1). As school leaders engage in decolonizing work they are able to add to this drawing on their lived experiences and research.

Engage in Self-reflexivity in Relation to Coloniality

Asher (2005) suggests that decolonization is a self-reflexive process requiring the deconstruction of not only the systems of the colonizer and external oppressive structures, but also one's own internalization of and participation in same. To engage in decolonizing education educators must reflect Educators reflect on their understanding of coloniality and how it is manifested in education and schooling. This might involve also a

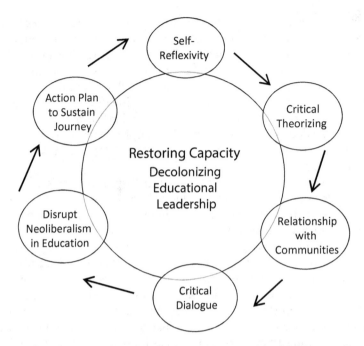

Fig. 5.1 Restoring capacity: Decolonizing educational leadership

process of decolonizing the mind, shedding colonial ways of thinking in relationship not only to education but other aspects of society. Through self-reflexivity educators acknowledge what they need to learn and unlearn. Self reflexivity allows White educators to examine how they have benefitted from privilege, begin to acknowledge their privileged position as settlers, and ways that they might be intentionally or unintentionally complicit with white supremacy. Critical educators are often reminded that educational experience and change is never about intent but impact. This process must be intentional and might evoke feelings of denial, anger, shame, guilt, dissonance, and resistance (Robbins & Jones, 2016).

Absolon (2012) suggests all journey focused on dismantling systems of oppression and decolonization begins with self, taking time to reflect and grow in one's identity before engaging in decolonizing education. As school leaders examine their lived expereiences they are forced to confront colonization and its impact not only on their lives but the lives of students they serve. Through the examination of experiences educators are able to explore ways of healing and new forms of knowledge. It is a process where educators come to understand what they need to learn and unlearn. It is also a space where some educators begin to acknowledge their privileged positions and their complicity in colonial practices. Through self-reflexivity educators begin the journey of understanding how colonialism continues to operate in daily life. They deepen their understanding of their own complicity with these and other colonial discourses and regimes of truth as they seek to work in ethically informed and relational ways. Self-reflexivity helps to dislodge ways of Western epistemic norms that have devalued other ways of knowing and open spaces for learning and relearning.

Through critical reflection educational leaders examine what they bring to their roles as leaders, including their personal histories (Lopez, 2015) their hidden beliefs and assumptions they hold about students are interrogated. Examining the inner self and relations to the world and the community is important to how school leaders alook at the education of young people. Self-reflexivity might also include a process of deconstruction and reconstruction as new knowledge is gained. Deconstruction is the process of tearing down old practices and reconstructing is the process of rebuilding with new knowledge. This level of critical consciousness guards against engaging in superficial and neoliberal forms of education that merely scratches the surface and brings about no real change. Becoming an educator committed to decolonial praxis is developmental and long term, a process that leaders must invest time and patience in as they examine how their identities connect to coloniality of power (Garcia & Natividad, 2018) and knowledge. Only when educators become morally and professionally committed to inclusive practices, to embrace difference and reflect on their own complicity in historical and contemporary discourses of colonization and oppression, will education and schooling be transformed (Lopez, 2019).

Develop Understanding of Critical Theorizing

Leaders grounding their work in a decolonizing approach must develop a cogent understanding of critical educational theories, in addition to decolonizing theorizing. The notion of critical that is used here means challenging dominant ideolgies and practices in education and schooling and supporting students to develop critical and political consiousness in regards to their environment and context. Critical theories include theories such as critical race theory, culturally responsive leadership, anti-racist education,

Black feminist theorizing, and other theories that challenge all forms of oppression. Critical theories inform decolonizing practice, in particular those focused on challenging systemic racism and white supremacy settler colonialism. Educational leaders should find areas of convergences and synergies between critical theories. Leaders are encouraged to learn about settler colonialism in all its forms, and take steps to address its negative impact on the distribution of land, water, and earth (Tuck & Yang, 2015); this includes historical examination of schools and school leadership. In Canada for example this means understanding the atrocities that occurred to Indigenous people in residential schools and the goals of the Truth and Reconciliation Commission of Canada (TRC) and ways that anti-Black racism and anti Indigenous racism are embedded in schooling practices.

Educational leaders should also be able to articulate points of departure and divergences between critical theories and articulate why decolonizing education advances their philosophy of education and educational outcomes they would like to achieve. In addition to developing a sound understanding of critical theories and decolonizing education, educational leaders must be able to connect theory to practice. They must be able to answer: *What does decolonizing educational leadership looks like and feels like in schools?* School leaders are encouraged to build a solid theoretical framework, and then build out from there to action. Actions might include working with teachers to develop decolonizing curricula assessments, a decolonizing approach to discipline, allocating resources to the library to obtain books that challenge coloniality and written by scholars from the Global South and so forth. Actions also include how they critically engage in the act of leadership at the personal level—dialogue, build trusting relationships, hiring, deal with conflict and resistance. Actions taken depend on context and where leaders are on their journey, recognizing that four hundred years and more of colonization will not be undone overnight. Environments must be created where teachers, students, parents, and communities are able to question the underlying assumptions of circulating discourses about curriculum and mobilize their own agency (Ylimaka, 2011).

Build Relationships Across Communities

Communities are inextricably linked to the schooling process, and as such leadership happens not only in schools but the wider community it serves. Education and community cannot be separated and school leaders have a central role in leveraging community resources for the academic success of students (Henderson & Mapp, 2002). Settler colonialism is ever present in communities through the occupation of land, language, and culture and ways that communities understand themselves and the world (Tuck & Gaztamide-Fernandez, 2013). It is important that school leaders become aware of the role and power of the community to change the schooling experience for students. Communities must be engaged if decolonizing efforts are to be successful.

Communities must be involved in the school decision-making process and the voices and experiences of elders and parents must be embedded in deep and meaningful ways. Educational leaders must be willing to learn from the community thereby disrupting Western epistemological systems. This creates opportunities for reconceptualizations of practice that foreground notions of identity, culture, and place (Carjuzaa & Ruff, 2010). School leaders engaging in decolonizing educational leadership must work to uplift communities and foreground the inextricable link between schools and communities. There must be respect and shared understanding. Responsive community school leaders play an important role in supporting student achievement and success and draw on community support to advance teaching, learning, and leadership (Gutiérrez, 2006).

Leadership should be of service to be service communities. A decolonizing approach calls for leaders who are committed to collaborative decision-making not only within the institutions of work, but also with local communities. Leaders as they engage with communities are encouraged to rethink their own definitions of success, advancement, and development, as it might be different from that of the community (Garcia & Natividad, 2018).

Engage in Critical and Difficult Dialogue

Critical dialogue is a form of "democratic practice, engagement, problem-solving, and education involving face-to-face [or via various technology platforms] facilitated ...discussions occurring over time" (Schoem, 2003, p. 216). Critical dialogues can be used to examine differences or develop shared understandings. Critical dialogues can also be used to develop relationships between different cultural groups, examine issues of power, privilege, and oppression toward a goal of individual and/or social change (Laman, Jewett, Jennings, Wilson, & Souto-Manning, 2012). Laman et al. (2012) suggest critical dialogue supports the "discursive work of praxis that involves constructing, deconstructing, and reconstructing knowledge of status quo discourses" (p. 199). When educators engage in critical dialogue they draw on their own narratives and that of others.

The work of Freire (1970) advancing the notion of critical consciousness has informed understandings of critical dialogue. School leaders are always in conversation with staff, students, the wider organization, and community. For example, in Ontario, Canada, school leaders might be in conversation with teachers at their school, and educators at school board level, and the Ministry of Education officials. These conversations can sometimes be challenging as leaders who are operating through decolonizing framework theory might challenge practices of teachers and others that do not challenge coloniality, but perpetuate practices steeped in colonial notions of power and knowledge. Educators are encouraged to plan for these dialogues, have resources available, and avoid spirit injury to themselves and others Spirit injuries are those wounds that hurt the soul, takes time to process and heal. Engagement in critical dialogue does not mean having all the answers, but a willingness to challenge the difficult, build relationships, and seek input from critical friends.

Through critical dialogue school leaders examine policies and practices. Building communities of practice create space to see where changes are needed to enhance a decolonial project at school level or system level. Conversations must not promote deficit notions about students and families but are proactive in challenging specific practices. In my own work and from research with school leaders notion of how 'to call out' and 'call in' during colleagues dialogues emerged. 'Call out' does not have to be instant, but necessitated when ideas and/or practices are harmful to students or others in the space. 'Call in' is seen as invitation to someone to join a critical dialogue. 'Call in' can be with people who hold similar views or with those who hold differing views with the intention of seeking understanding and engaging in disruption. Dialogues are no longer limited to face-to-face interactions, but can occur through various medium. Time, space, and texts (including technology and social media) play role-critical dialogues (Laman et al., 2012).

Disrupt Neoliberal Educational Policies

Colonial remnants continue in education in the discourses of educational policies and neoliberalism (Shahjahan, 2011). Neoliberalism is a socioeconomic theory that rejects governmental intervention in domestic economy and promulgates materialism, consumerism, and the commodification of public goods (including education), and is also a powerful force that has come to dominate the discourse and behaviors of many aspects of life (Giroux, 2004). Neoliberalism privileges the interests of private property owners and multinational corporations over the interest of society, attempting to bring all action under the rule and force of the market (Harvey, 2005). Some have linked neoliberalism with decreased state funding for education at all levels. Under neoliberalism everything is for sale or is plundered for profit including education and continues to be challenged all over the globe by students, labor organizations, intellectuals, community activists, and a host of individuals and groups who are unwilling to allow democracy to be bought and sold (Giroux, 2019).

Some see neoliberalism in culture as well, where the ruling class seeks to have their values and views as the norm. (Giroux, 2019) sees this as hegemony which seeks to disrupt the idea that people, particularly oppressed people, can construct their own alternate realities and who come to see their interests as lying with that of the ruling class. Giroux, 2019 and others suggest that this is often a hidden process that impacts our consciousness and the choices we make.

Under neoliberalismand neoliberal educational polices no longer is education seen as a social good with intrinsic value, but instead it has been reconceptualized as a commodity that a student purchases for his or her own gain (Rhoades & Slaughter, 2004). Adding to this hegemonic idea is also the notion that educators should be neutral disseminators of content information and should not bring their political views into the classroom. Some attack public intellectuals who posit empowering pedagogies and argue that educators should be neutral providers of decontextualized information and not seek to as they say 'indoctrinate' students. It is suggested by some that classrooms and indeed all of education should be political free zones. Apple (2004) argues that educating neutrally is a type of indoctrination and carries a lot of power and suggests that classrooms are inherently political. Some argue that students are impacted by neoliberal polices, where students become and are seen as consumers seeking to purchase education for the betterment of self. Scholars contintue to research the impact of neoliberalism on education in areas such as students, funding, curriculum, pedagogy, and programs. School leaders who embrace decolonizing leadership might find constant dissonance with educational polcies that they have to work with as most are framed within neoliberal norms. Decolonzing educational leaderdship is ongoing disruption and school leaders seek out space for agency and action where possible.

Action Plan to Sustain the Journey

Theory without practice remains inert knowledge. It is important for school leaders engage in critical models of leadership so that others can learn from it (Jean-Marie & Normore, 2010). Through action educational leaders exercise agency and carve out space to make a difference. As educational leaders work to engender change in the lives of marginalized students, developing agency means seeking out opportunities within education contexts to act collaboratively with others (Lopez, 2016). Decolonizing leadership must be translated to practice in order to create change and a clear action plan supports the process and journey. School leaders are encouraged to create an action plan for themselves on how action plans on how they will implement change, resources needed, and how actions will be evaluated to see impact and areas for change. Action plans must also include accountability for school leaders and educational leaders themselves, the system and those thosse they lead. Engaging in action takes time and norms disrupted. Some activists call for immediate action. gvien the violence that some students ans staff continue to experience in schools as a result oof white supremacy - and argue against the notion of a journey and time to change. These varying approaches signal the complexities of education and schooling in contemporary times. Educational leaders and practitioners have been trained to pathologize students behavior, instead of challenging the behaviors of the organization (Bensimon, 2012). Action plans must include ways to hold the system accountable instead of seeing students as the problem School leaders are encouraged to use race-based data to create programs for students and employ critical data interpretations. Taking action will require goal-setting exercises, data monitoring, and ongoing reflection (Malcom-Piqueux & Bensimon, 2015). Garcia and Natividad (2018) suggest:

> that leaders focus first and foremost on deconstructing their own leadership processes, in leading through a lens that is conscious of colonialism and white supremacy, adopting critical theories for leading, disaggregating data to reveal inequities, and engaging in consensus-building decision-making and action. (p. 34)

To alter educational outcomes for particular groups of students who are marginalized based on aspects of their identities, educational leaders whose practice are framed by decolonizing education must develop a plan to create the desired change. Sustainable change will not occur by itself but through commitment action (Lopez, 2016).

CONCLUSION

School leaders must be supported to challenge coloniality, colonial power, and knowledge. Supports can be provided through mentoring and critical friends. Colonial power takes effect in the present through the persistence of colonial discourses and practices. In order to decolonize education, educators must shift this thinking so that BIPOC BIR students can be free from hegemonic colonial knowledge and practices. Drawing on Battiste who suggests Battiste (2000) suggests "the purpose of Indigenous education is to help the individual become a complete man or woman. The goal is completeness" (p. 184). Decolonizing educational leaders embrace a view of learning that includes a holisitic approach and especially for students on whom the system inflicts violence urgeent action must be taken. Education should aim to benefit the entire child and in doing so will allow them to flourish, not only economically but more importantly holistically. In order to decolonize education, we must also look at ways in which coloniality of power and knowledge continue to be manifested in schools a theme threeoughout this book. Battiste (1998) suggests that any attempt to decolonize ourselves and actively resist colonial paradigms is a complex and daunting task. Education should make space for partnerships with Indigenous people in the process of decolonizing education. Leadership practices in the West and many countries in the Global South have been grounded in Western colonial knowledge. Decolonizing leadership reframes the premise of leadership by challenging this framework.

REFERENCES

Absolon, K. (2012). *Kaandossiwin: How we come to know*. Halifax, Nova Scotia: Fernwood Publishing.

Asher, N. (2005). At the Interstices: Engaging Postcolonial and Feminist Perspectives for a Multicultural Education Pedagogy in the South. *Teachers College Record* 107(5): 1079–1106.

Apple, M. (2004) *Ideology and curriculum*. New Yoek: Routledge.

Battiste, M. (1998). Enabling the Autumn Seed: Toward a Decolonized Approach to Aboriginal Knowledge, Language, and Education. *Canadian Journal of Native Education*, 22 (1) 16–27.

Battiste, M. (2000). *Reclaimining Indigenous voices and vision*. Victoria, BC: University of British Colombia Press.

Bensimon, E. M. (2012). The equity scorecard: Theory of change. In E. M. Benisimon & L. Malcom (Eds.), *Confronting equity issues on campus: Implementing the equity scorecard in theory and practice* (pp. 17–44). Sterling, VA: Stylus.

Carjuzaa, J., & Ruff, W.G. (2010). When Western Epistemology and An Indigenous Worldview Meet: Culturally Responsive Assessment in Practice. *Journal of the Scholarship of Teaching and Learning* 10(1) 68–79.

Craig, G. (2010). Community capacity building: Critiquing the concept in different policy contexts. In S. Kenny & M. Clarke (Eds.), *Challenging capacity building* (pp. 41–66). New York: Palgrave Macmillan.

Dinham, F., & Crowther, S. (2011). Sustainable school capacity building—One step back, two steps forward? *Journal of Educational Administration, 49*(6), 616–623.

Eade, D., & Williams, S. (1995). *The Oxfam handbook of development and relief.* Oxford: Oxfam.

Fanany, I., Fanany, R., & Kenny, S. (2010). Capacity building in Indonesia: Building what capacity? In S. Kenny & M. Clarke (Eds.), *Challenging capacity building* (pp. 156–184). New York: Palgrave

Freire, P. (1970). *Pedagogy of the Oppressed.* London and New York: Penguin Book.

Freire, P. (1972). *The pedagogy of the oppressed.* Harmondsworth: Penguin Books.

Fullan, M. (2006). *Turnaround leadership.* San Francisco: Jossey-Bass.

Garcia, G. A., & Natividad, N. D. (2018). Decolonizing leadership practices: Towards equity and justice at Hispanic-Serving institutions (HSIs)s and emerging HISs (eHSIs). *Journal of Transformative Leadership and Policy Studies, 7*(2), 25–39.

Giroux, H. (2004). Cultural Studies, Public Pedagogy, and the Responsibility of Intellectuals. *Communication and Critical/Cultural Studies* 1(1) 59–79.

Giroux, H. (2019). Neoliberalism and the weaponising of language and education. *Race and Class,* 61 (1) 26–45.

Gutiérrez, K. (2006). White Innocence: A Framework and Methodology for Rethinking Educational Discourse. *International Journal of Learning,* 12, 1–11.

Harvey, D. (2005). *A brief history of neoliberalism.* Oxford: Oxford University Press.

Henderson, A., & Mapp, K. (2002). A New Wave of Evidence: The Impact of School, Family and Community Connections on Student Achievement. National Centre for Family and Communty Connections with School.

Hill, P. W. (1997). *Towards high standards for all students: Victorian Research and Experience* (IARTV Seminar Series No. 61). Victoria: IARTV.

Jean-Marie, G., & Normore, A. (2010). *Educational Leadership Preparation Innovation and Interdisciplinary Approaches to the Ed.D. and Graduate Education.* New York: Palgrave Macmillan

Laman, T. T., Jewett, P., Jennings, L. B., Wilson, J. L., & Souto-Manning, M. (2012). Supporting critical dialogue across educational contexts. *Equity & Excellence in Education, 45*(91), 197–216.

Lopez, A. E. (2015). Navigating cultural borders in diverse contexts: Building capacity through culturally responsive leadership and critical praxis. *Multicultural Education Review,* 1–14.

Lopez, A. E. (2016). *Culturally responsive and socially just leadership: From theory to.action.* New York, NY: Palgrave Macmillan.

Lopez, A. E. (2019). Addressing Diversity in Schools Within a Global Context: Exploring Transformative Decolonizing Leadership Approaches and Practices. Paper presented at Korean Association for Multicultural Education. Seoul, South Korea, May.

Lopez, A. E., & Rugano, P. (2018). Educational leadership in Post-Colonial Kenya: What can we learn from the experiences of three female principals in Kenyan secondary schools? *Education Sciences, 8*(99), 1–15.

Malcom-Piqueux, L., & Bensimon, E. M. (2015). Design principles for equity and excellence at Hispanic-serving Institutions. San Antonio TX: HACU. Retrieved from https://vtechworks.lib.vt.edu/handle/10919/83015

Mitchell, C., & Sackney, L. (2000). *Profound improvement: Building capacity for a learning community.* Lisse, The Netherlands: Swets & Zeitlinger.

Pence, A. (2015). From capacity building to capacity promotion. In A. Pence & A. Benner *Complexities, capacities and communities: Changing development narratives in early childhood education, care and development* (pp. 7–15). Victoria, BC: University of Victoria.

Rhoades, G., & Slaughter, S. (2004). *Academic capitalism in the new economy:* Market state and Higer education. John Hopkins, Baltimore: John Hopkins University Press.

Robbins, C. K., & Jones, S. R. (2016). Negotiating racial dissonance: White women's narratives of resistance, engagement, and transformative action. *Journal of College Student Development, 57*(6), 633–651.

Schoem, D. (2003). Intergroup dialogue for a just and diverse democracy. *Sociological Inquiry, 73*(2), 212–227.

Shahjahan, R.A. (2011). Decolonizing the evidence-based education and policy movement: Revealing the colonial vestiges in educational policy, research, and neoliberal reform. *Journal of Education Policy* 26(2) 181–206.

Stoll, L. (2009). Capacity building for school improvement or creating capacity for learning? A changing landscape. *Journal of Education Change, 10*(2), 115–127.

Tedmanson, D. (2003, July). Whose capacity needs building? Open hearts and empty hands: Reflections on capacity building in remote communities. Paper presented at the *4th International Critical Management Studies Conference,* University of South Australia, Adelaide, Australia. Retrieved from https://pdfs.semanticscholar.org/41be/a00d729177fc98e93e2c015ee6773e2d3075.pdf

Tuck, E., & Gaztamide-Fernandez, R. (2013). Curriculum, Replacement, and Settler Futurity. *Jouranl of Curriculum Theorizing,* 29 (1) 72–89.

Tuck, E., & Yang, K. W. (2015). Decolonization in not a metaphor. *Decolonization: Indigeneity, Education & Society, 1*(1), 1–40.

Wenger, E. (1998). *Communities of practice.* Cambridge: Cambridge University Press.

CHAPTER 6

Recentering and Reconnecting: Creating Space for Renewal

Abstract This chapter explores the importance of educational leaders recentering and reconnecting to their own histories in decolonizing educational leadership. It draws on the work of Linda Tuhiwai Smith who posited the 'twenty-five projects' to support Indigenous research in ethical and responsive ways, and Maxine Greene in examining how imagination and envisioning supports educational leaders to seek out alternative approaches. Healing is an essential aspect of decolonizing work no matter the context and approach, which and includes leadership. The chapter concludes by exploring Willie Ermine's notion of 'ethical space' as a space for dialogue and healing.

Keywords Recentering • Reconnecting • Ethical space • Storytelling • Remembering • Reading • Envisioning • Creating • Pedagogy of resistance

INTRODUCTION

Engaging in decolonizing education should be a period of renewal, restoration, and hope. It is about finding new leadership approaches for engaging students, communities, and educators in transformative change. The undergirding philosophy is that the vestiges of colonialism continue to be present in education and schooling in the West and in the Global South.

© The Author(s), under exclusive license to Springer Nature   69
Switzerland AG 2020
A. E. Lopez, *Decolonizing Educational Leadership*,
https://doi.org/10.1007/978-3-030-62380-7_6

Coloniality—a reflection of colonialism—informs knowledge production and practices in education and power continues to be exercised through white supremacy and hegemonic relations. Decolonizing approaches reconnect people with their history drawing on their ontological experiences to inform educational practice.

In order to engae in this kind do praxis which is challenging on mind, body, and spirit, given the contemporary contexts the importance of recentering and reconnecting with one's history, the land, spirituality must be signaled as an essential ingredient and part of what sustains people on a decolonizing education journey. I share these notions drawing on my own ontological experiences, and the experiences of school leaders that I conducted research with. Participants shared ways in which their spirituality supported them on their educational journey and helped them to navigate educational contexts that were sometimes very challenging. A pedagogy of recentering and reconnecting can be embraced by educators no matter their race or other aspects of identity or social location.

One of the impacts of colonization is the damaging of the spirit and the minds of those they subjugate. This tyoe of subjugation also happens to students education and schools in the West as well as the Global South. Linda Tuhiwai Smith (1999)—a Maori scholar from New Zealand— reminds us that the impact of colonization was the "stripping away of *manza* (our standing in our own eyes), and an undermining of *rangatiramtanga* (our ability and right to determine our destinies)" (p. 173). Decolonization education is about resisting the ways in which colonial education separates the body from the mind of educators and positions knowledge as emanating only from the external. By recentering and reconnecting there is an acknowledgment that there is much to be learned from our histories that colonizers seek to deny through built in white supremacy education.

Engaging in decolonizing education means addressing the site and impact of colonial rupture. This includes the genocide of Indigenous people, the enslavement of African peoples, and all other people who experience subjugation. A robust naming of the brokenness in our bones will open doors to conversations and communities (Nahar, 2020). By recentering and reconnecting educators can examine the ways that colonial thinking, racism, and cultural appropriation have seeped into their thinking and practice. (Nahar, 2020). It is important in decolonizing work to recognize the emotional toll involved in resisting, and to take care of self and others. Decolonizing education to be successful must involve the collective. Recentering and reconnecting is about caring of self and others. In schools teachers must create safe learning environments for students, and those in formal leadership roles must create space to be in dialogue with those that they lead.

Recentering and reconnecting involve challenging, representation, imagery, and language that perpetuate white supremacy and colonial relations. It rejects the valorization of whiteness, and white desirability standards (that leads to toxic practices like skin bleaching), and recognize these ideologies as legacies of colonialism and enslavement. These messages are important for educators engaged in decolonizing education. Schools more than any other space where young people are gathered do harm to and BIPOC children's sense of self and identity. It is important for those who live in spaces that were once colonized and where "coloniality of power and knowledge" operates to keep subjugated people from their histories, to recover those histories through dialogue, oral histories, and through engagement with, and dissemination of, alternative histories and reject Eurocentric distortions of our histories (Racial Justice Network, 2020). Recentering and reconnecting is a means through which we challenge coloniality. This is a collective effort to reclaim space, knowledge, and all that was ruptured and taken. In North America and across the globe there is collective effort by oppressed people to challenge coloniality and white supremacy. Nahar (2020) notes:

> Decolonial struggles happening across North America [and globally] are the coordinated freedom efforts led by people who are current colonial subjects, in the sense that they are *subjected* to the dominant social system, and whose freedom the dominant system diminishes/rejects. The dominant system we have in the United States and Canada is one of cisheteronormative white supremacist, extractive capitalist patriarchy and it is a direct descendent of modern colonialism–the Christianized western European apparatus of tributational world governance.... This tributational system includes the people considered peripheral; they must defer to news, language, and cultural ways of the metropol over their own local coverage (and self-determination is ultimately oppressed). (p. 2)

Decolonizing education is a collective effort of all subjugated people to be free. Smith (1999, 2012) posits twenty-five decolonizing projects that invite Indigenous and non-Indigenous people to take up Indigenizing and indigenist processes, by "centring the consciousness of the landscapes, the images, languages, themes, metaphors, and stories of Indigenous world" (2012, p. 147). In some countries such as Canada, Australia, New Zealand, and the United States, where Europeans settled and stole the land, the term 'Indigenous' is used to describe native people who lived on those lands before the arrival of the settlers. I draw on Purcell (1998), as cited in Karanga (2019), who defines the term 'Indigenous People' as including

> [a] diverse group of people defined by the criteria of ancestral territory, collective cultural configuration and historical location in relation to the expansion of Europe. As existing descendants of non-Western peoples, Indigenous people have continued to occupy their ancestral lands after conquest by Westerners, and in some cases comprise people who have been relocated forcibly in the process of colonization. (p. 46)

While diversity exists in Indigenous communities, there are commonalities and shared experiences with people on the African continent, Australia, New Zealand, Canada, United States, and elsewhere, such as land, ways of knowing, and cultures being taken and destroyed by occupiers and settlers. Karanga (2019) applies the term 'Indigenous' to all people of African ancestry irrespective of their degree of proximity to the state of being colonized as well as the original inhabitants of lands of Canada.

As a person of African descent, an immigrant from Jamaica to Canada, it is important for my own existence and survival in this world to reconnect with the customs and history of the people of continent of Africa. As a descendant of the enslaved, I cannot name the country or countries where my ancestors were forcibly removed from, but the words of Marcus Mosiah Garvey, Jamaican National Hero and Pan Africanist: "A people without the knowledge of their past history, origin and culture is like a tree without roots." Engaging in decolonizing and decolonial education has given me an avenue to recenter and reconnect with the histories and traditions of my African ancestry which is central to who I am. Battiste (2013) captures these sentiments when she writes:

> Theorizing oppression and the deconstruction of educational histories of my people and the patterns of Eurocentrism and the decolonizing strategies in education have been my most productive writing moments as I drew on a growing number of Civil Rights and human Rights authors who were inspiring to me. As the balance of disciplines began to shift in education from modernistic expository prose of grand narratives to more

storytelling, to personal narratives and postcolonial analysis of colonization, to research on one's own perspectives, I took greater delight in reading and writing and found that the shift had brought my own analysis into
a different light. (pp. 16–17)

Academic institutions (schools and higher education) built on white
supremacy, and colonial power and knowledge, are spaces that continue to
injure and require performativity by Black, Indigenous and People of
Color (BIPOC) to survive. Reconnecting and recentering in the knowledge and history of my ancestors sometimes feels like a protective armor.
As Battiste (2013) notes, she does not recall much of her Eurocentric
schooling but what was important was her own path "toward understanding the collective struggles of Indigenous peoples framed within a patriarchal, bureaucratic enterprise of government, with education used as the
manipulative agent of various intended outcomes, some well-intentioned,
some not, but all strategic" (p. 17). This is indeed liberating for critical
educators seeking to use research, teaching, and scholarship to disrupt
coloniality. In the section below I frame recentering and reconnecting as a
pedagogy of resistance and hope for educational leaders.

Recentering and Reconnecting Leadership Pedagogy

In this chapter I position recentering and reconnection pedagogy as a
'form of pedagogy of resistance.' In other words, educators can learn and
utilize recentering and reconnecting as pedagogical tools in their leadership approaches that educators engaging in decolonizing education can
draw on, and in particular school leaders who are in constant and ongoing
relationships with students. While there are varied understandings of the
meaning of pedagogy it is generally understood to be the art and science
of teaching. As an educator and professor I engage in pedagogy in various
ways—through text, dialogue, stories, music, and so on with the aim of
supporting students to gain deeper understanding of issues and apply that
understanding in their own contexts and lives.

I draw on the work of Latin American scholars and others to postition-
ing Pedagogies of Resistance within decolonizing educational leadership
theorizing and practice. Pedagogies of resistance emerged from the struggles of critical scholars in Latin America and elsewhere. Jaramillo and
Carreon (2014) describe pedagogy of resistance as reciprocity, solidarity,
and democratic and horizontal decision-making structures. Resistance

pedagogies support social movements, and create space to critique and act upon inequities and the effects of capitalism on people's economic liveli-hood. Pedagogies of resistance seek "to undo the legacy of colonial-capi-talism and demonstrate a pronounced attempt to delink from the conceptual apparatus of neoliberal subjectivity altogether" (Jaramillo & Carreon, 2014, p. 395). Pedagogies of resistance builds on Freire's (1970) notion of critical education where students develop awareness of social inequalities in society that impact their lives and their communities.

As an educator I feel that knowledge must be applied and not remain in the realm of theory. One my educational journey as I gain deeper under-standings of the ways in which injustices are perpetuated in education and schooling my own pedagogy has evolved to reflect critical approaches to teaching, as a secondary school teacher, teacher educator, and professor of educational leadership. This positions teaching a space of resistance and critical work. As a critical educator I ask: *What does this feels like and looks like in practice?* In much the same way I hope educational and school lead-ers who frame their leadership approaches within decolonizing discourses will ask: *What does this feels like and looks like in how I engage in leadership?* In that sense recentering and reconnecting can offer new learning and pedagogies of leadership.

Louie et al. (2017) define remembering as connecting to what has been lived, and connecting as being in "communion" with all our relations. These include storytelling, restoring, discovering, sharing, reframing and revializing all imporant ingredients in renewal of not only spirit and body, but practice—as educational leaders our practices are not disconnected from the self. Opening up space in leadership discourse and practice for practices grounded in such as storytelling, restoring, discovering, sharing, reframing, and revitalizing add new dimensions to what it means to lead. By centering these practices, educational leaders create opportunities for students to utilize storytelling in their schooling experiences, furthering their growth and advancing their learning (Blakesley, 2010). Marsh and Croom (2016) argue that storytelling and counter-storytelling are central to decolonial praxis. Decolonization requires coexistence through diverse ways of living and thriving in the world. This means stepping away from hegemonic forces of colonialism and finding new pathways to resurgence by unlearning, reenvisioning, and recreating (Mignolo, 2011). According to Todd (2018), "decolonization can emerge through engaging with sto-rytelling to combat an education system that fails to fully engage in dia-logical modes of teaching and learning; by re-examining conceptions of times not as something that is linear; but cyclical; and by moving away from thinking in binaries that fail to serve us. Decolonization can thrive through Indigenous knowledges and an active reconnection with them.... Decolonization also involves seeking to address the ongoing injustices that colonialism has reproduced and continues to reproduce" (p. 190).

In outlining a research agenda, one that reclaims, reformulates, and reconstitutes indigenous cultures and languages with the strategic and relentless pursuit of social justice, (Smith, 1999) posits what she describes as 'twenty-five projects.' The projects Smith notes "are not claimed to be entirely indigenous or to have been created by indigenous researchers. Some approaches have arisen out of social· science methodologies, which in turn have arisen out of methodological issues raised by research with various oppressed groups. Some projects invite multidisciplinary research approaches. Others have arisen more directly out of indigenous practices" (p. 142). *The projects include claiming, testimonies, storytelling, celebrating survival, remembering, indigenizing, intervening, revitalizing, intervening, revitalizing, connecting, reading, writing, representing, gendering, envisioning, reframing, restoring, returning, democratizing, networking, naming, protecting, creating, negotiating, discovering, and sharing.* The 'projects' are not to be ranked or placed in hierarchical lists; they inform each other. While all of the 'projects' posited by Smith (1999) apply in some way to decolonizing education and leadership examining explicating all are outside the scope of this book. Those that I have used in my own pedagogy and decolonizing leadership approaches, as well as those that emerge from research with school leaders as offering support on their journey, and allowing them to recenter and reconnect are expanded upon. As such I explore storytelling, remembering, creating, reading, and envisioning in this chapter.

Storytelling

As mentioned above storytelling has been an integral part of my own life and family experience growing up in Jamaica. It is a tradition that I have passed on to my daughter, nephews, and granddaughters. Smith (1999) suggests "storytelling, oral histories, the perspectives of elders and of women have become is an integral part of all indigenous research and I add to all those seeking to connect with their histories and engage in new ways of engaging in education. Each individual story is powerful. But the point about the stories is not that they simply tell a story, or tell a story simply. These new stories contribute to a collective in which every person has a place. For many indigenous writers stories are ways of passing knowledge generations will treasure and pass on. The story and the story teller both serve to connect the past with the future, one generation with the other, the land with the people and the people with the story" (p. 145).

Storytelling happens through dialogue and conversations and is part of oral traditions of people of African descent and other communities. As Smith (1999) notes, storytelling is also about humor and gossip and creativity. The stories tell us about our cultures which can affirm us and also point to areas for further research and practice. Stories also help to create shared understandings and histories.

School leaders are encouraged to create the space and environment where students' stories form part of the curriculum and their teaching and learning experience. School leaders are also encouraged to find the stories that have informed their own lives and use these to inform how they engage in leadership. "One of the aims of decolonial thinking and decolonization is to re-instate, re-inscribe and embody the dignity, equity and social justice in people whose norms and values as well as their nature, their reasoning, sensing and views of life were 'violently or devalued or demonized by colonial, imperial and interventionist agendas" (LeBeloane, 2017, p. 1).

Remembering

Remembering relates not so much to an idealized remembering of a golden past but more specifically to the remembering of a painful past and, importantly, people's responses to that pain (Smith, 1999). People of African ancestry, remember the pain of our ancestors being forcibly taken from the continent, the suffering they endured in the 'crossing,' and the atrocities they endured at the hands of colonizers. This history is a powerful vehicle for change, but is also painful. Anti-Black racism is rooted in slavery. While the atrocities of slavery are painful to remember, Black people have drawn on this history to fight for change. Similarly, Indigenous people continue the fight for their land and their voices to be heard against regimes in various countries who refuse to acknowledge their rightful ownership of the land that settlers occupy. Smith (1999) asserts this form of remembering is painful because it involves remembering not just what colonization was about but what being dehumanized means for our own cultural practices. Both healing and transformation become crucial strategies in any approach which asks a community to remember what they may have decided unconsciously or consciously to forget.

School leaders must ensure that they understand their own histories and the histories of students and they are reflected in the curriculum. In Canada for example there are calls to decolonize the curriculum. Decolonization of the curriculum necessitates a rewriting of texts and curriculum materials that have been ignored for years, as well as showing settler colonizers in the true light through the violence they inflicted across the globe, enslaving native peoples, and stealing land and not as the romanticized conquerors and 'father' of civilization they have been portrayed as in texts. School leaders have access to resources, are in decision-making roles, and should make decolonizing of the curriculum and supporting teachers to engage in decolonizing praxis a priority.

Creating

Smith (1999) suggests that the project of creating is "about transcending the basic survival mode through using a resource or capability which every indigenous community has retained throughout colonization—the ability to create and be creative" (p. 154). Creating is not just about material objects but also about building in communities. Smith (1999) argues "that imagination enables people to rise above their own circumstances, to dream new visions and to hold on to old ones. It fosters inventions and discoveries, facilitates simple improvements to people's lives and uplifts our spirits" (p. 154). Colonial knowledge, power, and practices have the potential of sapping the creative energy from Black, Indigenous, and People of Colo through schooling and education. School leaders have a role to play in embracing policies that support the creativity of themselves, those that they lead, and students. Creating is about channeling collective creativity in order to produce solutions to indigenous problems. Throughout the period of colonization indigenous peoples survived because of their imaginative spirit, their ability to adapt, and to think around problems (Smith, 1999).

Reading

The history taught in schools in North America and other former colonized countries, is a misrepresentation of history and must be revised. Critical rereading of Western history and the indigenous presence in the making of that history has taken on a different impetus from what was once a school curriculum designed to assimilate indigenous children (Smith, 1999). On the continent of Africa and countries like Jamaica, religion and education were and continue to be intertwined with education as an ongoing colonial project. New reading programs must be motivated partly by a research and a need to understand what has informed both internal colonialism and new forms of colonization.

> The genealogy of colonialism is being mapped and used as a way to locate a different sort of origin story, the origins of imperial policies and practices, the origins of the imperial visions, the origins of ideas and values. These origin stories are deconstructed accounts of the West, its history through the eyes of indigenous and colonized peoples. The rereading of imperial history by post-colonial and cultural studies scholars provides a different, much more critical approach to history than was previously acceptable. It is no longer the single narrative story their way through undiscovered lands to establish imperial rule and bring civilization and salvation to barbaric savages who lived in utter degradation. (Smith, p. 146)

This notion of rereading is important in rethinking leadership appraoches and strategies in schools—the books that are tossed out, new materials acquired, the stories that are told. Educational leaders and school leaders have a role to play in creating the enviroment and school milieu for these kinds of actions. Leadership theories must be reread and shifted away from 'great men theories,' much of what students learn in history must be reread.

Envisioning

Maxine Greene (1995) encouraged people fighting for their justice to imagine a future they would like from the difficulties of their lives. She argued that social imagination is the capacity to invent visions of what should be and what might be in our deficit society, and that we must take action to repair and renew. Decolonizing leadership is about action and renewal. Leaders must be able to reimagine education and schools where the vestiges of colonialism and coloniality are no longer present. This kind of envisioning is possible through reconnecting and recentering oneself in their history and culture. Greene also noted:

> We also have our social imagination: the capacity to invent visions of what should be and what might be in our deficient society, on the streets where we live, in our schools. As I write of social imagination, I am reminded of Jean-Paul Sartre's declaration that "it is on the day that we can conceive of a

different state of affairs that a new light falls on our troubles and our suffering and that we decide that these are unbearable" .... It is out of this kind of thinking, I still believe, that the ground of a critical community can be opened in our teaching and in our schools. It is out of such thinking that public spaces may be regained. The challenge is to make the ground palpable and visible to our students, to make possible the interplay of multiple plurality of consciousnesses—and their recalcitrances and their resistances, along with their affirmations, their "songs of love." And, yes, it is to work for responsiveness to principles of equity, principles of equality, and principles of freedom, which still can be named within contexts of caring and concern. The principles and the contexts have to be chosen by living human beings ...using their imaginations, tapping their courage to transform. (Greene, p. 197)

Smith (1999) like Greene suggests envisioning as one of the twenty-five projects or methodologies in decolonizing education which asks that people to imagine a future, that rise above present-day situations and dream a new dream and set a new vision. As Smith (1999) suggests, some of the visions which bring people have passed down through generations as poems, songs, stories, proverbs, or sayings, used frequently in Indigenous and other societies where sayings, predictions, riddles, and proverbs are debated frequently and raised both informally and formally to guide practices and behaviors. The Jamaican culture is filled with proverbs, riddles, and sayings that have come down through generations and are essential to what it means to be Jamaican. These proverbs and riddles help students and school leaders to reconnect to their past histories and recenter their mind, body, and soul. Instead of being on the periphery of teaching and learning these riddles and proverbs should be at the heart of learning. The projects that Smith outlines connect well with my own positionality as a Black woman of African descent whose grandmother's stories were a staple and guiding force in my life and all her grandchildren's lives. These stories were passed down to her and represented our African history. They have allowed me to reconnect with the stories of my ancestors and have grounded how I walk in the world. My grandmother and elders in the community would share Anancy stories. There is an Anancy story to describe every situation. Anancy stories originated in West Africa and were brought to Jamaica by Ashanti slaves. These West African folklore focuses on the interaction between divine and semi-divine beings, royalty, humans, animals, plants, and seemingly inanimate objects. These stories continue to provide a moral foundation for the community (Auld, 2007).

Imagining and envisioning are central to educational theorizing and practice and is essential for decolonizing educational leadership. Ways that educational leaders can reimagine and envision leadership practice grounded interconnects with the suggestions for restoring capacity as highlighted in Chap. 5. What is being called for in decolonizing educational leadership is a radical way of leading schools that disrupts current practices such as school dicipline, engagement with community, intentionally challenging anti-Black racism, anti-Indigenous racism, and other forms of oppression—not just intentionally challenging but creating possibilites so that teachers and students can fully understand the history that gave rise to these forms of oppression. The activites that occur in schools must change—superficial celebrations that celebrate difference without challenging white supremacy must end.

ETHICAL SPACES

Space must be created in schools to allow leaders to recenter and reconnect, charting new ways of leading and supporting students. Space where colonizing practices are disrupted and new ideas about leadership and other aspects of schooling posited and acted upon. Where there is a genuine examination of "whose knowledge is included, whose languages are considered legitimate vehicles for carrying the knowledge, who are the people making these decisions, how will their choices be made, and what governs those choices, what is the role of critical education about the hierarchy of power embedded in society, and how can the inclusion of antiracist, anti-oppressive education support all students, not just Aboriginal ones?" (Battiste, 2013, p. 105).

Ermine (2007) theorized the notion of 'ethical space' as a space that connects Eurocentric and Indigenous knowledge systems. In Ermine's theorizing this is not a space of conflict necessarily, but a space where ideas are exchanged, and dialogue occurs about assumptions of values and interests this could be imagined as space where 'allies' and 'co-conspirators' have dialog conversations and plan action. The work of dismantling white supremacy is not the work of only BIPOC peope, but white allies and co-conspirators—it is a collective effort. In this space for example, Indigenous and non-Indigenous people begin to truthfully speak of the predicaments and issues that face them. Ermine suggests the ethical space is formed when:

two societies, with disparate worldviews, are poised to engage each other. It is the thought about diverse societies and the space in between them that contributes to the development of a framework for dialogue between human communities. The ethical space of engagement proposes a framework as a way of examining the diversity and positioning of Indigenous peoples and Western society in the pursuit of a relevant discussion on Indigenous legal issues and particularly to the fragile intersection of Indigenous law and Canadian legal systems. Ethical standards and the emergence of new rules of engagement.... (p. 194)

Ermine theorized the notion of the 'ethical space' to respond to the legal system and the ways in which Indigenous people were being treated by the courts in mush the same way critical race theory (CRT) emerged from the legal profession. He saw it as a way of bringing people with different understandings in dialogue. Educational leaders might use this approach as they are seeking to engage communities that have been marginalized by the school system. It could also be used in dialogue with students and staff. The 'ethical space' is envisioned in this work as space of healing for leaders and others. Ethical spaces can support reconnecting and recentering and as a space of reconstructing.

CONCLUSION

Decolonizing educational leadership is theorized as a process over time that call on leaders to develop leaders skills, to collaborate, and support others as well as reinvigorate self. This new approach to leadership grounded in decolonizing understanding evolves as school educational leaders hone their skills undergirded by a critcal understanding of needed changes and intended outcomes. As we embark on this journey we must find spaces to heal the colonial wounds that are not only in our past, but present in our everyday experiences. I see hope, promise, and transformative actions in a decolonizing approach and framework not only for self, but for other educators as well, and the ability to define one's own agenda for a new future.

REFERENCES

Auld, M. (2007). *The Anansi stories as mythology.* Retrieved from http://anan-sistories.com

Battiste, M. (2013). *Decolonizing education: Nourishing the learning spirit.* Vancouver, BC: Purich Publishing.

Blakesley, S. (2010). Storytelling as an insightful tool for understanding educational leadership in indigenous Yukon contexts. *Canadian Journal of Educational Administration and Policy.*

Ermine, W. (2007). The ethical space of engagement. *Indigenous Law Journal,* 6(1), 193–204.

Freire, P. (1970). *Pedagogy of the oppressed.* New York: Continuum.

Greene, M. (1995). *Releasing the imagination: Essays on education, the arts, and social change.* San Francisco, CA: Jossey-Bass.

Jaramillo, N., & Carreon, M. (2014). Pedagogies of resistance and solidarity: Towards revolutionary and decolonial praxis. *Interface: A Journal for and About Social Movements,* 6(1), 392–411.

Karanga, W. (2019). Land and healing: A decolonizing inquiry for centering land as a site of Indigenous medicine and healing. In N. N. Wane, M. G. Todorova, & K. L. Todd (Eds.), *Decolonizing the spirit in education and beyond: Resistance and solidarity* (pp. 45–64). Cham, Switzerland: Palgrave Macmillan.

LeBeloane, L. D. (2017). Decolonizing the school curriculum for equity and social justice in South Africa. *Koers – Bulletin for Christian Scholarship,* 82(3), 1–10.

Louie, D. W., Pratt, Y. P., Hanson, A. J., & Ottmann, J. (2017). Applying Indigenizing Principles of Decolonizing Methodologies in University Classrooms. *Canadian Journal of Higher Education,* 47(3), 16–33.

Marsh, T., & Croom, N. (2016). *Envisioning critical race theory in K-12 education through counter-storytelling.* Charlotte, NC: Information Age.

Mignolo, W. D. (2011). *The darker side of western modernity: Global futures, decolonial options.* Durham, NC: Duke University Press.

Nahar, S. (2020). Intersectionalization of the work that reconnects. *Deep Times: A Journal of the Work that Reconnects.* Retrieved from https://journal.workthatreconnects.org/2017/08/29/intersectionalization-of-the-work-that-reconnects/

Purcell, T. W. (1998). Indigenous knowledge and applied anthropology: Questions of definition and direction. *Human Organization,* 57(3), 258.

Racial Justice Network. (2020). *Principles for decolonial practice.* Retrieved from https://racialjusticenetwork.co.uk/2020/05/23/1066/

Smith, L. T. (1999). *Decolonizing methodologies: Research and Indigenous peoples.* London: Zed Books.

Smith, L. T. (2012). *Decolonizing Methodologies: Research and Indigenous Peoples.* London and New York: Zed Books.

Todd, K. (2018). Dreaming our way to new decolonial and educational futurities: Charting pathways of hope. In G. S. Dei & C. Jaimungal (Eds.), *Indigeneity and decolonial resistance: Alternatives to colonial thinking and practice* (pp. 183–214). Gorham, Maine: Myers Education Press.

CHAPTER 7

Conclusion: Looping Back and Moving Forward

Abstract This chapter points to the possibilities of decolonizing education and decolonizing educational leadership grounded in research and
scholarship, and my own journey of learning and unlearning. Drawing
on the work of Dei (2012) and his framework for Indigenous anti-
colonial knowledge as a way of exploring Black/African education in
diasporic contexts, I explore my own place within the context of Canada
as a Black Jamaican and descendant of the enslaved who were stolen
from the continent of Africa. There are aspects of decolonizing educational leadership that have not been explored that are beyond the scope
of this book such as an indepth examination of educational policies
within a decolonizing framework, leadership in higher education and so
forth. This main focus of the volume is leadership within K-12 schools.
These are however areas for further consideration within a decolonizing
framework. The chapter focuses on actions moving forward for educational leaders and concludes with hope and a call to action for all educators to resist dominant colonizing knowledge in order to transform
education and schooling.

Keywords Anti-colonial praxis • European colonization • Knowledge
production • Decolonizing curriculum • Policy • Indigenizing •
Western epistemologies • Resistance

This chapter loops back to Chap. 1 where the book startrd—grounded in my ontological and epistemological experiences as an educato and professor of educational leadership. Hence the metaphor "looping back and moving forward." As a Black woman, a descendant of the enslaved, and a Jamaican living in Canada, and an educator I continue to think about how I engage in critical education that disrupts the centrality of hegemonic colonial knowledge, make sense of my own lived experiences, and how this inform and contextualizes my work as a professor of educational leadership. Through this lens, I situate myself, interrogate my experiences in the education system in Canada, and develop theoretical perspectives that help me to account for my experiences. "Such perspectives must be rooted in our cultures, histories, and heritage and be presented as frames of reference for the intellectual and political projects of designing positive educational goals for learners" (Dei, 2012, p. 102). This book represents my frame of reference of educational and school leadership and informs ways in which I think the field might best move forward and respond to the needs of students, particularly those who have been marginalized by the education system. This chapter sets out the possibilities that I envision moving forward for the field of educational leadership. As a professor at a university steeped in colonial legacy, who conducts research individually and collectively, I am a producer of knowledge, and as such implicated in colonial power relations which means that I have a responsibility to consider the foundations and consequences of my work. I no longer willing to engage in work examine and disrupt colonial knowledge that is evident, not only in educational leadership but the entire educative enterprise. As education wrestles with current social and political shifts, and responds calls to address anti-Black racism, white supremacy, and all forms of oppression school leaders and all educational leaders must ask: *How can the field of educational leadership contribute to the task of dismantling white supremacy, dislodging anti-Black racism, and all forms of oppression, while at the same time advancing an agenda for education grounded in students' cultural knowledge and histories?* How can coloniality be disrupted in academia so that students and staff can exist without the harm and the need to perform and their knowledge can be accepted, valued, and included? The difficulty as Dei (2012) points out is how to do this? In the previous chapters I made some suggestions recognizing that there are multiple perspectives when it comes to decolonizing education, and that the work is incomplete and unfinished.

One cannot enter anti-colonial praxis with a colonized mind, recognizing that decolonization of the mind is an ongoing process. "As we seek to decolonize ourselves and the academy, we develop an anti-colonial intellectuality that helps us to challenge and subvert the colonial mappings and colonial cartographies of our institutions of learning …. Anti-Colonial intellectuality and praxis is about bringing ideas into fruition as social practice, as grounding and testing theories in the contexts of the liberatory struggles of our peoples as well as the people with whom we work" (Dei, 2012, p. 106).

European colonization left footprints on all aspects of our lives including education. European knowledge became the norm and informed the organization of social, economic, and political life in places that were once colonized and the effects continue today. Education and schooling today reflect these norms. White supremacy is a manifestation of that footprint. Decolonizing is about removing this footprint in education systems. This requires creating school systems that value and include the knowledge and experiences of all students. One of the effects of colonization was an education system that marginalized some students, particularly Black and Indigenous students. The lack of representation of Black and Indigenous bodies at all levels of education including higher education is a direct result of white supremacy, 'coloniality of power,' and knowledge that centers around Eurocentric knowledge. Coloniality and its impact is not always at the forefront of educational discourse. Space must be created for honest dialogue to happen, particularly around issues of race and blackness. As protests break out across the globe against racism some educational institutions are looking to decolonize the curriculum as they address racism and the lack of resources that reflect a more diversified population. Decolonizing is about the myriad of ways that colonialism is manifested in all aspects of life. Cruz (2012) suggests that decolonization is moving toward a different and tangible place and includes what Corntassel (2012) calls "everyday acts of resurgence."

The field of educational leadership continues to evolve in response to demographic changes, increasing diversity in schools, social and political shifts, and calls from communities and students who are not being served well by the education system. Research continue to show that Black, Indigenous, immigrant, and poor students are not faring well in schools in most Western countries because of systemic racism, discrimination, and other school practices. Those who lead schools must respond to the growing calls for more equity and justice in schools. We know from research that next to teaching, school leadership has the greatest impact on student outcomes. Leadership scholars and researchers over the years have focused on particular kinds of leadership to respond to the needs of a growing and changing student population. For example, culturally responsive leadership (Lopez, 2016), social justice leadership (Bogotch, 2002; Jean-Marie et al., 2009; Theoharis, 2007), and transformative leadership (Shields, 2011). How leaders address inequities, marginalization, advance social justice are common elements of these leadership approaches.

I posit decolonizing educational leadership as an alternative leadership approach that names coloniality and the impact of colonialism as factors that further inequities and marginalization of some students. It is the hope that school leaders might find it useful as they rethink their leadership approach, and add to their understanding of what it means to engage in decolonizing education. Central to this understanding and practice of leadership is the rejection of what Macedo (1999) refers to as "enslavement colonial discourse." This discourse permeates all aspects of education but has not been fully acknowledged in schooling practices as educators focus on equity, diversity, and social justice discourses that often do not name the ongoing impact of colonialism on education, and in particular leadership practices. Colonialism, and subsequently decolonization, has very real and material effects—we cannot forget this. These actions are held up by ways of thinking that disenfranchise, exploit, and marginalize Indigenous peoples and others around the globe (Ritskes, 2012).

Decolonization is not an event, but a process fraught with challenges. It is not romanticizing the past, but learning from it. Through hegemonic knowledge, and power colonial thinking continues to influence understanding of education and realities in many countries. This is what the decolonization seeks to address. Educational practices rooted in colonialism must be named and removed. Black Indigenous, People of Color parents want a curriculum that affirms their children and one that they can see themselves in. School leaders have a role to play in this; and the hope is that this book will contribute to that effort. Decolonization to be effective must be a complete project in schools that include leadership practices, curriculum, pedagogy, and overall school culture. There must be epistemic questioning of all knowledge and an interconnectedness built with Indigenous knowledge and learning in countries such as Canada. Battiste

(2013) suggests "Canadian administrators and educators need to respectfully blend Indigenous epistemology and pedagogy with Euro-Canadian epistemology and pedagogy to create an innovative ethical, trans-systemic Canadian educational system" (p. 168). From curricula to pedagogies, dominant knowledge systems have been organized and embedded through governing Eurocentric paradigms built historically within colonial specificities. Education systems and processes, as well as ideas about what counts as education, and knowledge have been entrenched in the reproduction of colonial ways of knowing which concomitantly limit possibilities for many learners (Dei, 2012).

As those in the field of educational leadership look to the future and intentionally work to dislodge colonial knowledge that informs many leadership practices in schooling today there are some areas of focus that should be addressed. These include educational policy, research in the Global South, principal preparation programs, and diversification of faculty in educational leadership programs at universities. Education policies do not normally tell you what to do; they create circumstances in which the range of options available in deciding what to do are narrowed or changed (Bell & Stevenson, 2015). Colonial practices in education are upheld by educational policies grounded in neoliberalism. For there to be material change in the lives of students, not only must policies change, but those who are involved in implementing them must also be involved in policy creation. The work of school leaders is shaped by and how they interpret, modify, or create policy at an institutional level. Moving forward it is imperative that school leaders become more aware of the impact of policy within decolonizing frameworks, and find space to disrupt policies that harm, perpetuate, oppression. Policy discourses provide educators with ways of thinking and talking about institutions to ourselves, and to others: In other words, they form a 'regime of truth' that "offers the terms that make self-recognition possible" (Butler, 2005, p. 22). Policy must be seen as discursive strategies—sets of texts, events, artifacts, and practices, that speak to wider social processes of schooling. This includes the production of 'the student,' the 'purpose of schooling,' and the construction of the 'teacher.' The discursive formation of the 'school' is that of a neoliberal institution (Ball, 2015). Educational policies do not exist in a vacuum; they are exercised within policy context and reflect the wider environment. Policy is political; it is about power determines what is done, and goes to the very heart of educational philosophy. Policies are seen as part of an analysis of change. Governments must be pressured to developing anti-colonial and decolonizing policies as those with power are often able to impact the policy-making process.

For colonial influence to be displaced from the field of educational leadership and decolonizing education take hold, the contexts of knowledge production must include research produced in the Global South and draw on Indigenous knowledges. The positioning of Western knowledge as the epitome of excellence and the continued questioning and positioning of knowledge produced elsewhere as not good enough and lacking in rigor, must end. In fact, the arrogance of scholars from the West, in particular White academics, who think they know more about the continent of Africa that Africans, is preposterous. Their claims are perfect examples of what Quijano (2007) describes as 'coloniality of power and knowledge.' They are steeped in neoliberal policies which are advanced through research and NGO's keeping many countries on the continent of Africa firmly in the grasp of former colonizers, and while they continue to dig out the resources for the benefit of former colonizers.

I am also suggesting that principal preparation programs and educational leadership programs foreground decolonizing educational leadership. "With its historic roots in the Anglo-European Enlightenment, the modern university is the epitome of Western institutions, having played a key role in the spread of empire and the scientific study and colonization of Indigenous peoples and cultures" (Williams et al., 2018, p. 17). The movement to 'Indigenize' universities, curriculum, and programs bears similarities with broader anti-racist perspectives expressed by racial minoritized academics (Spafford et al., 2006). The history of the academy in Canada has been dominated by Western epistemologies that have devalued Indigenous ways of knowing as a matter of course. This institutional history has set grounds for continued marginalization of Indigenous communities, cultures, and histories (Battiste, 2013; Sensoy & DiAngelo, 2012). The well-being of Black, Indigenous, and People of Color (BIPOC) students has been compromised by the impact of colonization on processes and content in contemporary systems (Little Bear, 2000). "The tendency of most university instructors to employ methods of instruction firmly situated within the epistemological structure of the dominant culture exacerbates what, for many Indigenous students, [Black and other students of color say], is a lifelong process of institutional marginalization by and alienation from mainstream Western schooling.

It is important that this book concludes with a note of hope and optimism, because that is who I am even in the face of challenges—hopeful and optimistic, because hope for me is a vehicle for action. Education is the belief in possibilities. We must hold beliefs that education can be liberating (Battiste, 2013). We are going to either be complicit in allowing education continue to reproduce Western epistemologies and sustain coloniality and neocolonization or work to decolonize it. We must extricate ourselves from Euro-colonial modernity, and "each generation must come out of relative obscurity, discover its mission, fulfill it or betray it" (Fanon, 1967, p. 206, as cited in Dei, 2012). "We must continue to resist dominant and colonizing knowledges and knowledge production in order to transform our educational institutions ....Our education must make a difference and create space for learners to work with[in] communities" (Dei, 2012, p. 109).

We must move forward together knowing there are different entry points to the work of decolonizing, recognizing, and affirming what Battiste (2013) calls the 'learning spirit,' recognizing that learning is "holistic, a lifelong process, experiential in nature, rooted in Aboriginal [Indigenous and peoples] languages and cultures, spiritually oriented, is a communal activity, involving community and elders" (p. 181). Through decolonizing education and schooling, and resisting colonizing knowledge, we will secure a better future for our children. As Dei (2012) asserts we must avoid the Cartesian split of mind and body and acknowledge the power of our ancestral knowings in our struggle against oppression, drawing on intellectual agency of African peoples in providing education for their children, which is not simply attending school, "but it is learning about family, community, nature, society and the interconnections through everyday practices and social activities" (p. 115) as we build liberatory ways of education and schooling. I end this book with two quotes from Marcus Mosiah Garvey—Jamaican National Hero—whose work has inspired me my entire life:

A people without the knowledge of their past history, origin and culture is like a tree without roots
and
We are going to emancipate ourselves from mental slavery because whilst others might free the body, none but ourselves can free the mind

REFERENCES

Ball, S. J. (2015). What is policy? 21 years later: Reflections on the possibilities of policy research. *Discourse: Studies in the Central Politics of Education, 36*(3), 305–313.

Battiste, M. (2013). *Decolonizing education: Nourishing the learning spirit.* Vancouver, BC: Purich Publishing.

Bell, L., & Stevenson, H. (2015). Towards an analysis of the policies that shape public education: Setting the context for school leadership. *Management in Education, 29*(4), 146–150.

Bogotch, I. (2002). Leadership for socially just schooling: More substance and less style in high-risk, low-trust times. *Journal of School Leadership, 12,* 198–222.

Butler, J. (2005). *Giving an account of oneself.* New York: Fordham University Press.

Corntassel, J. (2012). Re-envisioning resurgence: Indigenous pathways to decolonization and sustainable self-determination. *Decolonization, Indigeneity, Education & Society, 1*(1), 86–101.

Cruz, M. R. (2012). Ni con dios ni con el diablo: Tales of survival, resistance, and rebellion from a reluctant academic. *Decolonization, Indigeneity, Education & Society, 1*(1), 141–157.

Dei, G. S. (2012). Indigenous anti-colonial knowledge as 'heritage knowledge' for promoting Black/African education in diasporic contexts. *Decolonization, Indigeneity, Education & Society, 1*(1), 102–119.

den Heyer, K. (2015). An analysis of aims and the educational 'event'. *Canadian Journal of Education, 38*(1), 1–27.

Fanon, F. (1967). *Black skin, white masks.* New York: Grove Press.

Foucault, M. (1986). Of other places. *Diacritics, 16*(Spring), 22–27.

Jean-Marie, G., Normore, A., & Brooks, J. (2009). Leadership for social justice: Preparing 21st century school leaders for a new social order. *Journal of Research in Educational Leadership, 4*(1), 1–31.

Little Bear, L. (2000). Jagged worldviews colliding. In M. Battise (Ed.), *Reclaiming, Indigenous voice and vision* (pp. 77–85). Vancouver, BC: UBC Press.

Lopez, A. E. (2016). *Culturally responsive and socially just leadership: From theory to action.* New York: Palgrave Macmillan.

Macedo, D. (1999). Preface. In L. Semali & J. L. Kincheloe (Eds.), *What is Indigenous knowledge? Voices from the academy.* New York and London: Falmer Press.

Quijano, A. (2007). Coloniality and modernity/rationality. *Cultural Studies, 21*(2–3), 168–178.

Ritskes, E. (2012). What is decolonization and why does it matter? *Decolonization, Indigeneity, Education & Society, 1*(1).

Sensoy, O., & DiAngelo, R. (2012). *Is everyone really equal? An introduction to key concepts in social justice education.* New York: Teachers College Press.

Shields, C. (2011). Transformative Leadership: An Introduction. *Counterpoints, 409,* 1–17. Retrieved from http://www.jstor.org/stable/42981292

Spafford, M. M., Nygaard, V. L., Gregor, F., & Boyd, M. A. (2006). Navigating the Different Space: Experiences of Inclusion and Isolation Among Racially Minoritized Faculty in Canada. *The Canadian Journal of Higher Education, 26*(1), 1–27.

Theoharis, G. (2007). Social justice educational leaders and resistance: Toward a theory of social justice leadership. *Educational Administration Quarterly, 43*(2), 221–258.

Williams, L., Fletcher, A., Hanson, C., Neapole, J., & Pollack, M. (2018). *Women and climate change impacts and action in Canada: feminist, Indigenous and intersectional perspectives.* Canadian Research Institute for the Advancement of Women, the Alliance for Intergenerational Retrieved from http://www.adaptingcanadianwork.ca/criaw-acw-report-says-women-left-coming-renewable-energy-boom

Index[1]

[1] Note: Page numbers followed by 'n' refer to notes.

CPSIA information can be obtained
at www.ICGtesting.com
Printed in the USA
LVHW082303070723
751797LV00045B/15

9 783030 623791